UNITE History
Volume 3 (1945–1960)

The Transport and General Workers' Union (TGWU):
Post-War Britain, the Welfare State and the Cold War

UNITE History
Volume 3
(1945–1960)

The Transport and
General Workers' Union (TGWU):
Post-War Britain, the Welfare State
and the Cold War

Marjorie Mayo

LIVERPOOL UNIVERSITY PRESS

First published 2022 by
Liverpool University Press
4 Cambridge Street
Liverpool
L69 7ZU

British Library Cataloguing-in-Publication data
A British Library CIP record is available

ISBN 978-1-802-07710-0

Typeset by Carnegie Book Production, Lancaster
Printed and bound by CPI Group (UK) Ltd, Croydon CR0 4YY

Contents

Figures

Boxes

Acknowledgements

As the first chapter explains, each volume of this Unite History Project aims to co-research and co-produce political education resources, building on experiences of political education in the past, focusing on histories of collective action within a national framework. This has been a truly remarkable experience of teamworking. Appreciations are due to everyone who has contributed in their varying ways. Together we have been demonstrating ways in which oral histories can enrich the study of both published and unpublished materials, co-producing knowledge as the basis for collective learning for social transformation.

Particular appreciations are due, in addition, to John Fisher, the author of *Bread on the Waters*, the history of education within the T&G which provided so much of the material for Chapter 5, and to Adrian Weir who contributed to Chapter 2 as well as providing invaluable editorial support for the volume altogether. Many thanks to Ken Fuller and to Chris Wrigley too for their very helpful comments on an earlier draft.

Finally, many thanks to Unite and to the Marx Memorial Library for permission to reproduce images from their respective photograph collections. Unfortunately many of the images in their collections are undated. But these images do add to the text so they are very much appreciated even so.

Abbreviations

AACR	Association for the Advancement of Civil Rights
ABCA	Army Bureau for Current Affairs
BAME	Black, Asian and Minority Ethnic
BDC	Biennial Delegate Conference
BMC	British Motor Corporation
CIO	Congress of Industrial Organizations
CND	Campaign for Nuclear Disarmament
GCL	Gibraltar Congress of Labour
GEC	General Executive Committee
GPMU	Graphical, Paper and Media Union
ICFTU	International Confederation of Free Trade Unions
ISTC	Institute of Scientific and Technical Communicators
LGBT	Lesbian, Gay, Bisexual and Trans
LSE	London School of Economics
LTE	London Transport Executive
MCF	Movement for Colonial Freedom
MRC	Modern Records Centre, University of Warwick
NATO	North Atlantic Treaty Organisation
NATSOPA	National Society of Operative Printers and Assistants
NCCL	National Council for Civil Liberties
NCLC	National Council of Labour Colleges
NHS	National Health Service
NUPBW	National Union of Printing, Bookbinding and Paper Workers
NVV	Nederlandse Vuurtoren Vereniging
PPP	People's Progressive Party
REO	Regional Education Officer
SOGAT	Society of Graphical and Allied Trades
T&G	Transport and General Workers' Union
TGWU	Transport and General Workers' Union
TWI	Training Within Industry

WEA   Workers' Educational Association
WFTU   World Federation of Trade Unions
WVS   Women's Voluntary Service for Civil Defence

Foreword

Unite History Project
The Six-Volume History

2022 marks the centenary of the formation of the Transport & General Workers' Union (T&G), now a part of Unite, Britain and Ireland's largest union in private industry. The T&G was also a significant workers' organisation in public-sector employment, a tradition carried forward into Unite.

The T&G was the first general trade union, taking pride in organising workers in every occupation and delivering collective bargaining across a multitude of industries. The T&G held real industrial power through much of its history, and it was from this basis that millions of working people won better pay and conditions that dramatically improved living standards.

The union also exercised a great deal of political influence, particularly within the Labour Party. This and its interaction with government, often as a powerful independent actor in its own right, provide the setting for a wider chronological history of the labour movement in Britain – and to that extent also the industrial and political history of Britain; it was not without a significant impact in Ireland as well.

This history reflects and exposes the wider processes of social change in which working people played an active role, in terms of creating an understanding of oppression in society and exploitation, particularly of women and black people, in the workplace. In addition, the union's international work and campaigns are brought into sharp focus.

Many of the T&G's general secretaries, from Bevin to Morris, have been the subject of biographies, and Jack Jones published an autobiography. But this series is different: among other things it examines how the union's central function, campaigning and winning on jobs, pay and conditions, evolved over the course of the twentieth century.

This six-volume series tells this story in a highly original way, as it enables the incorporation of local history as played out by the union's shop stewards and branch officers. Work has been undertaken at regional level, based on interviews and newly uncovered archival material, that brings our history to life and gives a human dimension to an otherwise 'top level' narrative. Unions are after all composed of individuals – in the T&G's case, hundreds of thousands.

I believe that these volumes will make a great contribution to Unite's educational programmes with its members, workplace representatives and other activists, and more generally in colleges and universities; nothing like this work has been published before.

If we are to avoid the mistakes of the past it is of course essential that we understand and learn from it! This series of six books, detailing the history of one of the twentieth century's most important and vital trade unions, gives us that opportunity, and I commend them to you.

Sharon Graham
General Secretary
Unite the Union

1

The Context: Post-War Opportunities and Challenges

'No socialist who saw it will forget the blissful dawn of July 1945', enthused Michael Foot, 'eyes were fixed on the promise of a new society' with the election of the post-war majority Labour government. This marked the beginning of a new era, it was widely believed. 'Suddenly the vision of the Socialist pioneers had been given substance and historic impetus by the radical political ferment of wartime'.[1] Writing in *Tribune*, the radical Aneurin (Nye) Bevan, MP, expressed this enthusiasm in similar terms, pointing to the significance of the British people's vote for 'a new world, both at home and abroad'.[2]

This volume starts from this extraordinary moment in the trade union and labour movement's history. There were such high hopes for the future, with such determination to avoid the sufferings of high levels of unemployment that blighted the thirties. Popular support could be mobilised for new approaches to public policy, drawing on people's experiences of planning during the Second World War. And Labour leaders who had gained experiences of government themselves, as members of the wartime coalition, were in a correspondingly stronger position to make the changes that were so urgently needed. This context seemed to offer unique opportunities for the trade union and labour movement to move forwards towards Bevan's 'new world both at home and abroad'.

Or did it? This volume explores the challenges as well as the opportunities for radical reform as these played out between 1945 and 1960 (another watershed year as well as being the year of Bevan's own death). These were challenges and opportunities that needed to be addressed, both at home and abroad – with significant interconnections between the two in the context of movements for colonial freedom, all set against the background of the Cold War as this took off after the Second World War.

---

1 Michael Foot, *Aneurin Bevan, Volume 11, 1945–1960* (Granada, 1973), p.17.
2 Foot, *Aneurin Bevan*, p.18.

Subsequent chapters illustrate the remarkable achievements of this period, along with some of the period's shortcomings, including those relating to struggles for equalities, human rights and solidarity, both at home and internationally. There would seem potential lessons to be learned, reflecting on some of the parallels to be drawn, in more contemporary times. One of the key aims of this series of books is to do precisely this, to understand our past, in order to share learning together for the future.

The 1945 Labour Government: An Extraordinary Government in Exceptional Times

Overall, post-war Labour governments achieved so much,[3] despite the limitations of their times. By 1948 already the nationalisation proposals of the 1945 manifesto, 'Let Us Face the Future', had been carried out, including the nationalisation of the railways, along with coal, gas and electricity, most wharves and docks, London's buses and tubes and the Bank of England, (iron and steel was nationalised subsequently).[4] The National Health Service (NHS) had been established (despite the British Medical Association's opposition). And a new system of social insurance had been developed, ending the hated Poor Law of the past, as part of the establishment of Britain's welfare state. In the words of even such a robust socialist critic as Ralph Miliband: 'In housing, in education, in welfare, it (the Labour government) could well boast to have done more than any Government had done before – and to have done it in the midst of acute economic difficulties'.[5] The Britain of 1945 was far poorer than the Britain of today. And the country had been devastated by war. Yet so much was achieved. So how did this happen?

These were exceptional times – but in what ways? The first point to emphasise is that the trade union and labour movement had emerged from the Second World War in a relatively stronger position than before. There had been fears that the high levels of unemployment that had been experienced in the 1930s might return, but this did not happen. The immediate post-war years were characterised by relatively full employment. And full employment enables workers to organise with some confidence. So the trade union and labour movement was in a correspondingly more powerful position than had been the case during the depression of the inter war period. By the end of the Second World War Trade Union Congress (TUC) affiliate members numbered nearly seven million, with

3 Peter Hennessy, *Never Again: Britain 1945–51* (Penguin, 1992); Hugh Clegg, *A History of British Trade Unions Since 1889, Volume III 1934–1951* (Clarendon, 1994).

4 The Labour Party, '1945 Labour Party Election Manifesto' (1945), http://www.labour-party.org.uk/manifestos/1945/1945-labour-manifesto.shtml.

5 Ralph Miliband, *Parliamentary Socialism*. 2nd ed. (Merlin, 1972), p.286.

over eight million members of trade unions overall, surpassing the record membership of the immediate post-First World War period.[6] Trade union membership had increased even further to nearly 10,000,000 by the end of this period, in 1960.

The T&G was the biggest union with 1,271,000 members at the end of the Second World War,[7] including significant numbers of women. Women had been increasing in the union during the war years, increasing nine-fold to reach 306,707 by 1943,[8] demonstrating how effectively they could take on jobs that had previously been regarded as men's preserve. (The first T&G women's conference had taken place in that same year in 1943).

Most importantly too, the trade union movement had become recognised as a 'great and permanent estate of the realm' in the words of the historian, Peter Hennessy.[9] Even before the Second World War, T&G's Ernest Bevin had claimed that the TUC had virtually become part of the state, making its views heard at the highest levels. This may have been something of an exaggeration, it has been argued,[10] reflecting more about Bevin's aspirations for corporatism than the reality actually warranted. The trade union and labour movement did become far more closely engaged with the state as part of the war effort, however. This relationship has been described as an implicit contract. The trade union and labour movement had supported the war effort. But rewards would be expected just as soon as the war were to be won.[11]

This collaboration had included Bevin's own contributions as Minister of Labour and National Service in the coalition government from 1940. Trade unionists continued to play key roles subsequently. Six trade union leaders were included within Attlee's first cabinet, in 1945. Trade union representation on official bodies also increased over this period, from 60 to 81 official bodies, forms of representation that continued even after Labour's electoral defeat in 1951. One of the early symptoms of this changing context emerged with the repeal of the hated anti-trade union Trades Disputes and Trade Union Act, in 1946, for example, removing legal limitations that had been imposed in the aftermath of the General Strike.

Wartime experiences had then been significant in a number of ways. Labour leaders (including Bevin from the T&G) had gained direct experience of being in government. This had given them the knowledge and skills together with the confidence that being in government could impart. Most importantly too, the coalition government had taken on considerable powers for planning and direct intervention in the economy as part of the

6 Robert Taylor, *The Trade Union Question in British Politics* (Blackwell, 1993).
7 Clegg, *History of Trade Unions.*
8 Andrew Murray, *The T&G Story* (Lawrence & Wishart, 2008).
9 Hennessy, *Never Again*, p.69.
10 Taylor, *The Trade Union Question.*
11 Taylor, *The Trade Union Question.*

Ernest Bevin
(1881–1951)

Ernest Bevin was a co-founder of the T&G in 1922, as Volume 1 has already explained. He was general secretary of T&G from then on, until 1940, when he joined the wartime coalition, as Minister for Labour and National Service. Previous volumes have covered Bevin's contributions as a trade unionist, a staunch right-winger although committed to obtaining benefits for his members. He was followed, first as acting general secretary, and then from 1945 as general secretary, by Arthur Deakin, who shared Bevin's overall political perspectives.

Between 1940 and his death in 1951 Bevin's own contributions to the trade union and labour movement were mainly as a Labour politician (although he did return briefly to T&G after the war, in 1945, before joining Attlee's government). He had been seen as an effective minister during the war years despite having had very little formal education.

As foreign secretary under Attlee, Bevin played a key role in international affairs. During the war, he had celebrated the comradeship that had developed, especially the alliance between the United States, Russia and the British Commonwealth. 'Nothing gave me greater joy' he had told the T&G's biennial conference in 1943, 'than when on that wonderful day the Cabinet decided to accept the twenty years' treaty with Russia' (MRC, MSS.126/TG/1887/10, 10th Biennial Delegate Conference, 1943).

Once the war was over, though, Bevin's position was completely reversed. With the onset of the Cold War, he became passionately anti-Soviet. And pro the USA (although not entirely uncritically). He supported the development of the Marshall Plan to promote Western Europe's recovery, aiming to ensure that Western Europe would constitute a bulwark against what he perceived to be the threat of communism from the East. And he also contributed to the development of the North Atlantic Treaty Organisation (NATO).

Whilst Bevin had been critical of what he had described as Britain's 'scuttle' from India, he was also pragmatic about Britain's international role. For example, he supported Britain's departure from Palestine after the bombing of the King David Hotel, considering that the British Mandate for Palestine had become more trouble than it was worth. Chapter 3 explores these international issues in further detail.

Bevin died in 1951. At the biennial conference in Whitley Bay that year, tribute was paid to Bevin as follows: 'he *was* this Union' (MRC, MSS.126/TG/1887/14, 15th Biennial Delegate Conference, 1951). He was described as the creative genius and the dynamic personality that had welded together those unions which constituted the original amalgamation of 1922. A man of many achievements he has also been a deeply controversial figure in the history of the T&G.

war effort. Public opinion had come to accept such interventions in these exceptional circumstances. And the sky hadn't fallen in for capitalism. This meant that there was far more potential support for nationalisation than there had been previously. Peter Hennessy quotes the findings from a wartime survey of people's expectations for the post-war period, with 21 per cent looking for more state control, and 29 per cent looking for less class distinctions more generally.[12] So, this was a relatively favourable climate for socialist advance.

There was also widespread support for the establishment of the welfare state. Socialists had been drafting plans for a very different future. And William Beveridge (who was not a socialist himself, far from it, in fact) had been responsible for drawing up the Beveridge Report. This had gained widespread enthusiasm, promising to slay the giants of want, disease, ignorance, squalor and idleness, by providing the national insurance system, the NHS, secondary education, social housing and full employment for all. These plans for the welfare state had been discussed across the country, as well as being discussed within the armed forces as part of the forces' own education programmes via the Army Bureau for Current Affairs (ABCA), raising aspirations for the post-war period, both in Britain and beyond. In summary then, these were exceptional times. And they were exceptional for a number of reasons, preparing the ground for very different futures for the trade union and labour movement from 1945.

Whilst there were extraordinary opportunities, however, trade unionists shouldn't be too starry-eyed about Attlee's post-war Labour governments from 1945 to 1951. There were also powerful challenges to be faced. These challenges gathered momentum in the 1950s, under successive Conservative governments, setting the scene for the struggles that followed – and have continued to follow, in more recent times. More of which later.

Continuing Challenges for the Labour and Trade Union Movement

There were economic challenges and there were political challenges, both in Britain and internationally, with strong interconnections between them, at every level. Despite the achievement of full employment, as the country began the massive tasks of post-war reconstruction, economic problems began to emerge, right from the very start. Britain struggled to maintain its position as an imperial power, its economy weakened by the war effort, increasingly dependent on the United States. This was a very vulnerable position indeed, with major implications for both domestic options and for foreign policy options. And there was worse to follow.

The United States had provided economic support during the war, through the 'Lend-Lease'; this was an arrangement which had provided

12 Hennessy, *Never Again*, p.77.

Britain with much needed credit. But this support was rapidly cut off after the war, leaving the British economy in considerable jeopardy. As Peter Hennessy summarised the situation: 'We were, in short, morally magnificent but economically bankrupt as became brutally apparent eight days after the ceasefire in the Far East when President Truman severed the economic lifeline of Lend-Lease without warning'.[13] War 'socialism' could be built on, in Hennessy's view but was this enough to build the New Jerusalem, he questioned?

The abrupt termination of the Lend-Lease agreement meant that Britain was in desperate need of alternative sources of finance. The US was able to strike a hard bargain, as a result of Britain's vulnerability, providing low interest credit in exchange for Britain's agreement to allow holders of pounds sterling (which had been a tightly controlled currency) to convert these pounds sterling into dollars. And convert their holdings, the sterling holders proceeded to do – in significant numbers.

This might seem a technical issue, of interest primarily for financiers. But it was an issue with massive ramifications, described as a time-bomb ticking beneath the exhausted, depleted and overstretched British economy'.[14] The British economy became extremely vulnerable to sterling crises as a result of these arrangements, leading to the subsequent devaluation of the pound in 1949. This was the start of a series of problems for the longer term.

The post-war period became dominated by Exchequer anxieties about Britain's continuing role as international banker and the position of sterling, with continuing anxieties about rising inflation. Successive governments showed determination in their attempts to contain this by holding down wages and profits – except that policies became increasingly focused on the former, and correspondingly less focused on the latter. Trade unionists understandably wanted to know why workers were being asked to bear the brunt of the nation's economic difficulties. Conflicts over prices and incomes policies characterise the periods that followed, with massive implications for the trade union movement. These were themes that underpinned trade unions' relationships with subsequent governments, starting with the Labour governments from 1945 to 1951, and moving on from there during successive Conservative governments.

Nor were these the only problems to be faced. Far from it in fact. There had been underlying weaknesses in British manufacturing industry which faced even great struggles to be competitive in the post-war period. Britain hadn't been defeated or occupied during the war. It was ironic perhaps, but this turned out to have been a mixed blessing. Britain didn't

---

13   Hennessy, *Never Again*, p.94.
14   Hennessy, *Never Again*, p.98.

experience the pressures to modernise that impacted on their competitors across the Channel.

Meanwhile Marshall Aid from USA was providing much needed investment in the devastated economies of Western Europe – part of the USA's strategy to keep the region safe from communism as the Cold War developed in the post-war period (more of which later, in Chapter 3). These investments soon began to produce results. By 1956, for instance, West Germany had overtaken the UK in terms of producing and exporting cars; this would have been a major disappointment to the previous Chancellor of the Exchequer Stafford Cripps, who had hoped to increase car exports as part of his strategy for boosting the economy more generally. (Cripps died in 1952).

The failure to invest and modernise British industry has been another recurring theme, throughout this period and beyond, along with the dominance of finance capital, as later chapters also illustrate. These were problems that continued to bedevil the economy, as the trade union and labour movement's alternative economic and political strategy was arguing, over subsequent decades.[15]

Stafford Cripps (firstly president of the Board of Trade and subsequently Chancellor of the Exchequer between 1947–1950) had also identified the lack of professional planning expertise amongst British managers as another major weakness. (He did not support workers control – for the same reason – not being convinced that as yet a very large number of workers in Britain (were) capable of taking over large enterprises lacking the necessary education and skills in his view). The failures of management in the past had been key to the problems of the newly nationalised industries. The coal industry was a case in point. Nationalising coal was relatively uncontentious, for precisely this reason, it has been argued, the industry having suffered from decades of mismanagement and a continuing lack of investment. This was a lame duck industry waiting to be rescued by the state.

So how much difference did nationalisation actually make for the workforces in question? How far were management weaknesses resolved, with – or typically without – greater trade union involvement in strategic planning? Or to what extent did nationalised industries actually bear the brunt of government attempts to hold back wage demands? These are questions to be explored more fully in Chapters 2 and 6.

Meanwhile the coal industry also illustrates some of the wider problems that faced the Attlee government from its early days, compounded by problems in the transport industries. Fuel stocks proved totally inadequate in face of very severe weather in the winter of 1946–1947 as a result. This

15 Nicholas Costello, Jonathon Michie and Seumas Milne, *Beyond the Casino Economy* (Verso, 1989).

Figure 1: Clement Attlee at a T&G event

was not what nationalisation had been supposed to achieve. The difficulties in these industries may have effectively discouraged some of Attlee's ministers from pursuing further nationalisations subsequently, it has been suggested,[16] reinforcing the concerns of sceptics within the Labour government.

Ralph Miliband also focused on such differences of view about the future of further nationalisations. Whilst recognising and celebrating the achievements of Attlee's first government from 1945, Miliband pointed to the Party's relative weaknesses and internal divisions. The socialist credentials of Attlee's first government had always been contested in his view. There had indeed been activists for whom the reforms from 1945 were 'the beginning of the socialist revolution'.[17] But others (including many of the leaders) saw the reforms of these early years between 1945 and 1951 as the ultimate achievements, concluding that it was time for consolidation.

In the event, Labour lost the subsequent election in 1951, despite increasing Labour's share of the popular vote, handing political power back to the Conservative government of the former wartime leader,

16 Hennessy, *Never Again.*
17 Miliband, *Parliamentary Socialism*, p.307.

Clement Attlee
(1883–1967)

Clement Attlee came from a prosperous middle-class family; he was educated at a public school (Haileybury) and Oxford before training as a barrister. But he came face to face with poverty and deprivation as a volunteer in London's East End, experiences which convinced him of the case for socialism. He concluded that the state needed to intervene to promote social justice and human rights which could never be achieved by charitable interventions alone.

During the First World War he served in the army, after which he returned to work in the East End, becoming mayor of Stepney. Although he became a personal friend of the radical Labour Party leader George Lansbury (whom he succeeded as leader in 1935) Attlee was not so radical himself. But he was a conviction politician who could be persuaded to change his mind when presented with sufficiently compelling arguments. He became convinced of the case for Indian independence from British colonial rule, for example, although he had initially been opposed to this.

During the Second World War in 1940, Churchill invited Attlee and colleagues to join him in a national government, a coalition that survived until 1945, with Attlee as deputy prime minister from 1942. This experience of government stood him in good stead when Labour came to power afterwards, in 1945. He has been described as a great team player rather than a charismatic leader, a modest man who had 'much to be modest about' as Churchill is alleged to have quipped.

In government from 1945 to 1950 and again from 1950 to 1951, Attlee's Labour government carried out their election pledges, nationalising some 20 per cent of Britain's industry and establishing the main pillars of the welfare state, including the NHS. Whilst these were extraordinary achievements there is another side to the story, however. There were less radical aspects, both at home (with Attlee being prepared to send troops against dock workers on strike) and abroad, (with Attlee supporting the US in the Cold War against the USSR and its allies, although he was not a gung-ho Cold Warrior himself).

After Labour's election defeat in 1951, Attlee continued to lead the Labour Party until 1955, when he was succeeded by Hugh Gaitskell. There had been divisions throughout Attlee's time as leader. These divisions took on new forms under Gaitskell's leadership, with battles for the soul of the Labour Party as a result. Attlee himself struggled with ill-health in his later years, although he survived until 1967.

Winston Churchill. Subsequent Conservative governments accepted many, although by no means all, of the Attlee government's reforms. But they began to pursue increasingly determined attempts to push back on wages.

In contrast, the Labour Left continued to argue for radical policies, both at home and abroad, supported by the Left within the trade union and labour movement, including the Left within the shop stewards movement. There were tensions throughout this period then, with varying outcomes. And there were very different approaches to leadership within the trade union movement, as the story of the T&G itself illustrates, from Ernest Bevin and Arthur Deakin on the Right through to Frank Cousins and Jack Jones on the political Left. More of Arthur Deakin, Frank Cousins and Jack Jones subsequently.

Whilst the leadership of the T&G seemed to shift dramatically from the Right to the Left of the political spectrum in the post-war period, these shifts need to be understood within the context of continuing struggles, at different levels, from the shop floor upwards. Such political differences emerged in relation to trade union struggles on domestic issues, such as prices and incomes policies and pressures on wages and conditions more generally, along with shop-floor resistance to proposed job losses through industrial restructuring proposals. And they emerged in relation to international policies and their effects in the context of the Cold War.

Britain's Role in the World Following the Second World War

Britain had been on the winning side, an ally at the so-called 'top table', with Churchill sitting alongside US and Soviet leaders, setting the framework for the post-war settlement in Europe. As the leader of a global empire, Churchill expected Britain to continue to play a global role – on a commensurate scale. But to what extent were such aspirations at odds with reality? Britain 'was morally magnificent but economically bankrupt', failing to compete effectively with the rivals that had just been defeated so recently.[18] So how could Britain continue to punch above its (diminishing) weight?

One of the key challenges that Attlee faced, when Labour had defeated the Conservatives back in 1945, had related to Britain's imperial past. There were politicians of both parties who supported Britain's continuing role. And there were politicians – of both parties – who questioned this. Could Britain afford to hold onto its Empire without jeopardising its domestic recovery along with its commitment to public spending on the welfare state?[19] Were there hard choices to be made?

18 Hennessy, *Never Again.*
19 Hennessy, *Never Again.*

It was actually a Conservative prime minister, Harold Macmillan, who commissioned a cost benefit analysis of the Empire towards the end of this period, ushering in the 'winds of change' in terms of developments towards colonial freedom.

By that time (the end of the 1950s, when Macmillan was reflecting on the costs of Empire) the Indian sub-continent had long since gained independence, Attlee having been converted to the necessity of such a move in the immediate post-war period. But what about Britain's colonies elsewhere, particularly in Africa and the Caribbean? Could Britain manage without their contributions, providing raw materials on the cheap, along with their contributions in terms of providing manpower for the armed forces? And should it do so anyway? Some, including Bevin, had argued against what he termed the 'scuttle' from India, believing that there could be continuing partnerships between Britain and its colonies – for mutual benefit. But others took very different positions, supporting the case for colonial freedoms. Britain's changing role has involved significant implications for trade unionists internationally, as well as significant implications in terms of race equalities and anti-Semitism. (Anti-Semitic mobilisations in Britain increased again in the post-war period). There were implications both within and beyond the trade union and labour movement more generally.

Meanwhile relationships between the former victors of the Second World War had been deteriorating, with mounting suspicions that the Soviet Union was planning to invade Western Europe. Cold War paranoia began to spread, with massive consequences as a result. The United States became embroiled in McCarthyism, fearing communist infiltration, looking for reds under so many beds, both at home and abroad. The Marshall Plan had been specifically aimed to counter communist influence in Western Europe by providing economic aid, increasing US influence as a result. And in turn this growing influence impacted on Britain.

Britain was amongst the Western European countries to negotiate US support in the desperate days of 1947. Without US dollars, it was secretly calculated at the time, rations of 1,700 calories a day would be imposed, over 1,000 calories less than the minimum ration that had been calculated as necessary during the war.[20] But US dollars came at a price, with increasing US influence on foreign policy. The overall shift in world power that followed the Second World War impacted on Britain across different international spheres. Reflecting on changing relations in the Middle East in the early 1950s, for example, Macmillan pointed to 'the most noticeable, and painful difference between our positions now and when we were in office' (i.e. during the war) 'is our relationship to the US. Then we were on

20 Hennessy, *Never Again.*

an equal footing – a respected ally… Now we are treated by the Americans with a mixture of patronising pity and contempt'.[21]

Britain's changing relationship with the US constitutes a theme that runs throughout this period up to and including more recent times. This has been and continues to be highly contentious within the trade union and labour movement. There have been varying views on the so-called 'special relationship' along with varying views on Britain's efforts to maintain a position at the 'top table' internationally. This provides the context for subsequent debates within the movement as to whether Britain should have its own nuclear weapon, a bomb with 'a bloody Union Jack on top of it' in Bevin's view, if not an uncontentious one.

The Cold War impacted on the trade union and labour movement in so many ways, even if the worst excesses of McCarthyism began to tail off towards the latter part of this period. International trade union collaborations were deeply affected in the post-war period, with the development and subsequent sabotage of the World Federation of Trade Unions (WFTU). This had been founded in 1945 to support workers' rights internationally (although this didn't necessarily extend to the right to national independence from colonial rule in the view of some of the major players). But with the advent of the Cold War, the WFTU was split in 1949, a split that was triggered by T&G's Arthur Deakin, a determined Cold War warrior in his own right, a trade union leader who tended to identify – and blame – communists as being behind every strike. It was this anti-communism that was behind his walk out from the WFTU. The ramifications of this split impacted on the trade union movement in Britain, as well as internationally, including implications for the T&G in Gibraltar, a Cold War case study that emerges in more detail in Chapter 3.

The Cold War impacted on Britain in other ways too, with pressures for significantly increasing expenditure on defence. These pressures were exacerbated by the outbreak of the Korean War in 1950. Supporting the USA in this attempt to prevent communism from taking hold in the Korean peninsula proved both contentious and costly – and ultimately unsuccessful. The Korean War ended in stalemate. But far from leading to reductions in defence spending, it has been argued that this actually had the opposite effect. Both US and USSR upped their spending on nuclear weapons, working on developing the hydrogen bomb (the H-bomb) which would be even more destructive than the atomic bombs (A-bombs) that had been dropped on Hiroshima and Nagasaki at the end of the Second World War.

Britain came under pressure to increase its spending on rearmament too. Whilst Attlee went along with these pressures (even if reluctantly) others took very different views. Nye Bevan, the hero of the establishment

---

21 James Barr, *Lords of the Desert* (Simon and Schuster, 2018), p.150.

Aneurin (Nye) Bevan
(1897–1960)

Nye Bevan came from a coal mining community in South Wales, going down the pit himself in his teens. He became an active trade unionist, playing a leading role in the General Strike in 1926. As Labour MP for Ebbw Vale he went on to gain national prominence as a vocal critic of Churchill and the Conservatives more generally.

He was appointed Minister of Health in Attlee's post-war Labour government, playing a key role in the establishment of the NHS. This was a remarkable achievement, all the more remarkable for the determination with which Bevan faced down opposition from the British Medical Association. Bevan resigned in 1951 rather than agree to the imposition of charges on teeth and glasses in order to pay for increased expenditure on armaments.

Meanwhile Bevan's remit also included housing. He is famous for arguing that public housing should represent a positive choice, rather than a residual category to be reserved for the poorest in society:

> We should try to introduce in our modern villages and towns what was always the lovely feature of English and Welsh villages, where the doctor, the grocer, the butcher and the farm labourer all lived in the same street. I believe that is essential for the full life of citizen [...] to see the living tapestry of a mixed community. (Housing Bill, Second Reading: Hansard, HC Deb, 16 March 1949, vol. 462, cc.2121–231)

Some 850,000 homes were built in the four years immediately after the war ended –the biggest housing programme ever introduced. Although Bevan's rate of house building was subsequently overtaken, with 300,000 a year under Macmillan, this was at the expense of the quality of the homes being provided.

After Attlee's retirement in 1955 Bevan became first shadow colonial secretary and then shadow foreign secretary (in 1956). He was critical of Stalin, but he was not a Cold War warrior, questioning Britain's increasing reliance on the US. He expressed varying views on nuclear disarmament, coming out against unilateral disarmament eventually, thereby surprising some of his supporters on the Left of the Labour Party. His death, in 1960, was widely mourned.

of the NHS, resigned in 1951 over the financial implications of precisely this issue, when charges were imposed on teeth and glasses so that Britain could afford to spend more on arms. Defence spending continued to be contentious, throughout this period and beyond. There have been financial objections and there have been political and moral objections, particularly

Figure 2: Nye Bevan at a T&G event

evident in debates about nuclear disarmament in the latter part of this period. Taken together with the contested question of whether there should be further nationalisations, these debates have been described as a battle for the soul of the Labour Party by the end of the fifties. Before moving on to introduce the chapters that explore these and other themes, however, the following section summarises the key features of the context that faced the trade union and labour movement in 1945.

The Context in 1945 in Summary

This could be seen as a blissful dawn, raising hopes of building a new and fairer society in post-war Britain. The Labour government that won parliamentary power in 1945 started with unique advantages. A number of Attlee's ministers had experience of being in government. And there was relatively widespread acceptance of the case for state intervention to promote the nation's well-being. This included state intervention in the economy, as well as state intervention to develop the welfare state.

With relatively full employment, the trade union movement was in a correspondingly strong position. During the war, trade unions had gained far greater acceptance, in terms of their roles on official bodies. And membership had been increasing and continued to increase from the Second World War onwards. So far, so good.

But there were major challenges to be faced. The inherent weaknesses of the economy soon became only too apparent, including the weaknesses associated with Britain's financial role and the problems associated with defending the pound. This led to increasing pressures on trade unions to hold back on wage demands, pressures that were compounded by the trade union movement's relationships with Labour governments between 1945–1951.

Britain became increasingly dependent on its so-called 'special relationship' with the US in this context. This impacted on foreign policy in the Cold War period, with increasing pressures to spend on arms, thereby adding to the country's economic difficulties. These difficulties were further compounded by Britain's attempt to maintain its imperial role in the post-war period.

The trade union and labour movement was deeply divided on how to respond to these challenges. Were the reforms of 1945 just the beginning of longer-term processes of social transformation? Or was this enough? How should trade unions respond to calls to moderate their demands in the national interest, whether employers were being called upon to make similar sacrifices or not? What role should Britain play on the international stage and at what cost? And how might such decisions impact on struggles for equalities within the trade union and labour movement and the wider society? These debates run through the chapters that follow, raising questions for discussion about their continuing relevance in the contemporary context?

The Chapters That Follow

Chapter 2: Class Struggles in T&G from 1945 to 1960
This chapter explores the question of who should bear the brunt of Britain's economic problems in the post-war period. How do industrial struggles in this period illustrate the changing relationships between labour, capital and the state more generally, including the role of the law and legal rights? How far were trade unionists prepared to make concessions to a Labour government in the post-war context and for how long could such concessions hold on the shop floor? Should the trade union movement aim to become more firmly established as a 'great and permanent estate of the realm' (Bevin's view) – and what might have been the price of gaining and maintaining such a position? How different were trade unionists' relationships with Conservative governments – and how did such relationships develop over time?

These questions are explored through a number of case studies including case studies of strikes in transport industries such as the docks (where troops were used against strikers by a Labour government). There is also discussion of industrial action involving buses and trams, strikes in the motor industry over industrial restructuring and job losses and strikes in the print industry.

Chapter 3: International Solidarity – or Not
This chapter explores examples of international solidarity as well as reflections on cases where there was a lack of effective solidarity. These examples are set in the context of debates on Britain's imperial role, Marshall Aid, NATO and the Cold War, together with debates on the H-bomb and the 'battle for the soul of the Labour Party', in the latter part of this period.

This chapter also includes discussion of Arthur Deakin's role in undermining the WFTU together with a number of other examples to illustrate Deakin's role in the Cold War, including his role in undermining T&G organisation in Gibraltar.

Britain's international role as a former imperial power – striving to maintain its global position in straightened circumstances – had major implications, impacting on the economy as well as impacting on struggles against racism and anti-Semitism, struggles that are explored more fully in the following chapter. Before moving on to these struggles for equalities, Chapter 3 examines T&G's role in movements for colonial freedom and the Campaign for Nuclear Disarmament (CND).

Chapter 4: Struggles for Equalities
This chapter starts with discussion of the 1948 Nationality Act and the aftermath (with Attlee apparently revealed as being implicitly racist,

although anxious not to appear so). These issues are set are in the context of the Cold War, taking account of contentious issues about decolonisation and international solidarity (as raised in the previous chapter). Case studies include struggles against the Far Right and anti-Semitism in the post-war period, along with struggles against racism, including struggles against the colour bar.

The chapter then moves on to explore struggles for women's equality in the workplace. There were struggles for equal pay for equal work. And there were struggles for women to remain in the workforce at all, with discussion of attempts to squeeze women out of jobs after the Second World War, compounded by the closures of so many wartime nurseries.

The role of women's structures in the T&G emerge together with cross references to women's interests in trade union education, issues that are explored more fully in Chapter 5.

Chapter 5: Trade Union Education

This chapter focuses on trade union education as this developed during this period: education to produce more skilled negotiators and/or to produce more politically conscious activists, including women activists. Different approaches to education are considered, including different, more participative methods under Arthur Deakin and Frank Cousins.

John Fisher's book, *Bread on the Waters* starts with a preface by Jack Jones, summarising the importance of trade union education for all, from shop floor to those in senior positions. 'Knowledge leads to influence' and effectiveness.[22] There was major expansion and innovation between 1946 and 1959, according to Fisher, with different approaches to the overall aims as well as to the methods to be developed.

There were also shifts of approach in terms of the methods of learning that were to be applied. The emphasis was to be on active learning methods such as role play, focusing on relevance and practical applicability. As women's membership began to grow again after the war, women's education began to be taken more seriously too, with dynamic women playing leading roles.

To summarise the achievements in trade union education and the T&G during this period, Fisher compared the number of those in correspondence courses in 1948–1949 (1,583 students) plus 630 students who had attended day and weekend schools with the 19,154 T&G students on courses in 1955–1956.

22 John Fisher, *Bread on the Waters: A History of TGWU Education 1922–2000* (Lawrence & Wishart, 2005).

Chapter 6: Arguments for Democracy Within the T&G and Beyond
This chapter starts by focusing on struggles for democracy within the trade union movement – how should the T&G develop for the future? There were pressures for centralisation during Deakin's time as general secretary, attempting to manage unofficial/shop-floor militancy, leading to struggles that Chapter 2 has already outlined. Whose side are you on, trade unionists had asked of their leaderships in such contexts. In his autobiography Jack Jones raised similar questions about which side Deakin was on (in his view it was the employers). Jack Jones himself took a very different approach, building on Cousins's achievements as general secretary, giving far more weight to rank-and-file involvement, building trade union democracy from the shop floor upwards.

The chapter concludes by focusing on debates about what type of society the trade union and labour movement should be aiming to achieve for the future. And what, more specifically, should nationalisation be about? Should nationalisation set out to promote industrial democracy and socialism? Or should nationalisation simply aim to restore particular industries to profitability, part of a strategy to develop a more rationally planned economy. This relates to wider debates about the changing relationships between capital, labour and the state, together with wider debates about equalities and social justice both in Britain and beyond.

Questions for Discussion
Debates That Run Through the Chapters That Follow

- Whose side has the union been on, whether officially and/or unofficially, in different disputes over the years?

- How far should trade unionists go in making concessions to support a Labour government or the prospect of a Labour government?

- What can we learn about building solidarity, and promoting equalities, both internationally and more locally?

- How can the union be most effective whilst strengthening democratic accountability?

- How can union education contribute to the development of political consciousness as well as the development of specific skills?

Timeline of Key Events

1945

- Election of Attlee's Labour government
- A-bombs dropped on Hiroshima and Nagasaki by USA
- Truman ends Lend-Lease
- Unofficial dock strike: troops called in

1946

- Bank of England nationalised
- Trade Disputes Act repealed
- Fulton Speech opening up the Cold War

1947

- Coal and cable & wireless nationalised
- Marshall announces plan for aid to Europe
- Attlee announces austerity plan
- India becomes independent (followed by Partition massacres)

1948

- Railways and electricity nationalised

- Cold War purge of communists and fascists from 'sensitive' civil service posts

- Empire Windrush arrives in Tilbury

- NHS inaugurated

1949

- British Nationality Act comes into force

- Gas nationalised

- Troops go into Avonmouth, Liverpool and London docks

- Sterling devalued

- Agreement between government and trade unions on wages standstill

1950

- General election: Labour's majority cut

- London dock strike: troops move in

- British troops to be sent to Korea: defence estimates trebled

- Wage freeze breaks down

1951

- Iron and steel nationalised

- Repeal of Order 1305 banning strikes during the war

- Ernest Bevin dies

- Nye Bevan resigns over dental and spectacles charges

- US tests H-bomb

- General election: Labour loses, and Churchill becomes prime minister again

1952

- European Coal and Steel Community (forerunner of the European Union) set up

- TGWU Shop Stewards' Handbook produced

1953

- Stalin dies

- Armistice signed on Korean War

- First Cirencester summer school

1954

- Cabinet agrees to manufacture H-bomb

- Movement for Colonial Freedom (subsequently called Liberation) formed

- End of wartime rationing

1955

- Churchill resigns, succeeded by Anthony Eden

- General election: Conservatives win again

- Arthur Deakin (T&G GS) dies

- Attlee resigns as Labour leader: replaced by Gaitskell

1956

- Frank Cousins elected T&G general secretary

- Strikes in motor industry

- British (and French) troops invade Suez: resulting in debacle

1957

- Eden resigns: Macmillan succeeds as prime minister

- Strikes at post-war high

- First Aldermaston march

1958

- CND formed

- Racial disturbances in Nottingham and Notting Hill
- London bus workers strike

1959

- General election: Conservatives win again
- T&G passes motion against nuclear weapons
- Print strike

1960

- Macmillan delivers 'winds of change' speech on decolonisation
- Nye Bevan dies

2

Class Struggles in the T&G from 1945 to 1960

This chapter explores the changing relationships between labour, capital and the state from 1945 to 1960. This was a period in which the trade union and labour movement had significant advantages. The first post-war election had resulted in the victory of a Labour government in 1945, promising support for radical reforms including reforms to remove anti-trade union legislation from the statute book. The trade union and labour movement had been centrally engaged in the war effort, as active partners, with enhanced legitimacy as a result. Most importantly, in addition, unemployment was relatively low. There were labour shortages, as it turned out, as Britain began to tackle the devastation that had been caused by the Second World War. So labour was in a correspondingly strong position. This stood in contrast with the previous situation, in the immediate pre-war period, when widescale unemployment had undermined trade unions' bargaining power to a significant extent. So far so good then.

But the economy had structural weaknesses. There were major challenges as a result. British industry had been in need of modernisation for some time already. Critics, including critics on the Left, had been pointing to the problems arising from poor management and lack of investment in the mines, for example, problems that nationalisation was supposed to resolve, with public intervention as the remedy for the failures of the private sector. Was this actually about 'rescuing lame ducks' – lamed by poor management in the past in other words? What did nationalisation resolve in practice? How much difference did nationalisation actually make for the workers involved – either in the mines or elsewhere? And most importantly, how far were the workforces in these industries – or indeed in other industries – expected to bear the costs of modernisation in post-war Britain?

As the previous chapter has also outlined, the British economy became increasingly vulnerable for other reasons too, including its vulnerability to runs on the pound, the costs of trying to maintain Britain's imperial role with a 'seat at the top table', and the costs of defence spending as a result of the Korean War. Meanwhile the United States was investing in the economies of Britain's competitors via Marshall Aid in the context of the Cold War (striving to keep Western Europe 'safe from communism'). The British economy was struggling to keep up with these challenges.

There were dilemmas for the trade union and labour movement as a result. How far would trade union leaders be prepared to make concessions on issues such as prices and incomes controls in order to support the newly elected Labour government in the post-war context? The TUC and many trade union leaders initially supported the Attlee government's approach. Although Deakin himself was initially dubious about if not actually opposed to the notion of formal wage restraints in the immediate post-war period, by 1948 he had come around to the view that there were situations in which this could be justified. Although he had felt reservations about governments interfering in free collective bargaining, he became convinced of the need for a planned economy under a Labour government, with trade unions playing a 'responsible role' in managing wage pressures. There were real dilemmas here, whatever your view of Deakin's approach more specifically – how to distinguish the potentially fine line between supporting the case for socialist planning involving some restraint on all sides, on the one hand, versus accepting that the workforce should bear the brunt of the burden of change on the other.

This chapter starts by focusing on these relationships between the trade union and labour movement and Labour governments. How did such relationships between labour, the state and capital develop over time? This sets the scene for considering trade union relationships with the Conservative governments that followed. How far did these differ from their relationships with the Attlee governments? How did relationships with the Labour Party change following the shift to the Right with the election of Hugh Gaitskell as leader in the latter part of this period? And most importantly, how did trade unions themselves respond to these challenges in terms of developing their own strategies and modernising their own structures at this time?

As the previous chapter has already outlined, these questions are explored through a number of case studies. These include case studies of:

- disputes in nationalised industries where there was a significant level of state intervention, such as in the docks, road haulage and passenger transport industries

- strikes in the motor industry over industrial restructuring and job losses in the private sector (although there was some evidence of government interventions in the private sector too) and

- strikes in the print industry, where the print unions were developing more co-ordinated approaches to tackling issues of pay and conditions, including the campaign for the right to organise and the campaign for the 40-hour week as well as strategies to tackle divisions within the labour force, for the future.

Struggles in the Docks

One of the outcomes of the Second World War had been the establishment of the National Dock Labour Scheme from 1947. This reduced casualisation in the industry, guaranteeing dockers in the ports covered by the scheme payment for being available for work. This was a major step forward for a centrally important section of T&G, with some 85,000 members (65,000 of them in ports covered by the Dock Labour Scheme). The docks were serviced by 90 full-time T&G officials, with 34 others also dealing with the docks as part of their allocation of duties. And the National Dock Labour Scheme had equal representation from the unions' and employers' sides plus an independent chair.[1] Deakin himself referred to this as a form of workers' control. So far, so good then.

The reality was more complex, though, as it very soon emerged. The Dock Labour Scheme brought important benefits, providing dockers with guaranteed wages even when business was slack. When business was booming however, there were suspicions that the costs might be offsetting the benefits; the scheme could be seen as 'an excuse for the imposition of an onerous level of labour discipline' despite the level of formal trade union representation, as Andrew Murray has explained – 'like living under the Gestapo!' it was argued by rank-and-file trade unionists at the time.[2] This situation resulted in difficulties in some ports and a spate of unofficial actions, as Attlee's government was soon to appreciate. In addition, the situation in the docks was further complicated by the fact that there were thousands of dockers who belonged to other unions, with different traditions rooted in varying conditions, working with different types of cargo and varying port facilities. This was a context that was potentially rife with conflict.

For the newly elected Labour government, however, the docks absolutely had to operate smoothly. This was essential for the country's recovery. Any disruption in trade was presented as a national emergency, it was argued, with the use of the wartime legacy of emergency works orders, invoked by the Attlee government against peacetime industrial action in the docks.

---

1 Jim Phillips, 'Decasualisation and Disruption: Industrial Relations in the Docks 1945–79', in Chris Wrigley (ed.), *A History of British Industrial Relations 1939–1979* (Edward Elgar, 1996), pp.165–185.
2 Murray, *The T&G Story*, p.104.

The leadership of the T&G, under Deakin, was in agreement with the government's view on this. Attlee himself appreciated Deakin's support, describing him as a man who at all times 'showed great courage' adding that he was always resolute in the face of opposition.[3] Deakin has also been described as frowning upon almost any form of industrial action, and most especially upon unofficial action. As he was reported as arguing to the Scottish delegate conference in 1946, on the folly of unofficial action, 'unofficial strikes will not get us anywhere, rather they will land us into considerable trouble and difficulty'.[4] But unofficial actions were precisely what emerged, despite (or perhaps because of) the best offices of the large number of full-time officials allocated to them, officials who tended to be very loyal to the leadership that had appointed them[5] – and correspondingly distanced from their membership, it has been suggested.

Strong unofficial leadership emerged in response to this situation in the docks, especially in London and Liverpool. Rank-and-file trade unionists were coming up against their own leadership in the T&G, as well as challenging the newly elected Labour government over issues of pay and conditions. The first series of dock strikes took place in 1945, a strike over wages that lasted six weeks. Some 45,000 dockers were reported as being on unofficial strike at 13 ports, that October, with the strike still spreading. The men were reported as being 'weary of the slowness of the negotiating machinery', suspicious of the employers and apparently frustrated with the union.[6] The following day troops were brought in to start unloading ships carrying food supplies.

There were further disputes in 1948 (over the rate for handling a 'dirty' zinc oxide cargo in this particular case). Attlee himself outlined his views on dock strikes when he made a broadcast in the summer of that year, 1948, arguing that unofficial strikers needed to be reminded of the new duties that accompanied their new rights.

> This strike is not a strike against capitalists or employers. It's a strike against your mates. A strike against the housewife. A strike against ordinary people who have difficulties enough now to manage on a shilling's worth of meat and other rationed commodities. Why should you men strike? You're well paid, compared with the old days. You have a guaranteed minimum wage of £4 8s 6d a week whether you work or not.[7]

3 Geoffrey Goodman, *The Awkward Warrior: Frank Cousins: His Life and Times* (Davis Poynter, 1979), p.101.

4 Arthur Deakin 'Union Policy on Wages, Unofficial Strikes and the Closed Shop', in *The Record* (T&G, 1946), p.90.

5 Murray, *The T&G Story*.

6 Reported in the *Daily Worker*, Friday 12 October 1945, p.4.

7 Quoted in Peter Hennessy, *Having It So Good* (Penguin, 2007), p.24.

Arthur Deakin
(1890–1955)

Arthur Deakin was brought up in poverty in South Wales, leaving school at 13 to work in an ironworks. He became an active trade unionist, joining the docks union that became part of T&G. His experiences as a trade unionist have been described as somewhat limited, however; he was not associated with any major strike movements, his view of trade unionism being formed by Ernest Bevin's more bureaucratic, corporatist approach to industrial relations. Jack Jones subsequently described Deakin as being somewhat in the shadow of Bevin, his predecessor as general secretary.

Deakin has been described as obsessively anti-communist, looking for reds under every bed, convinced that every strike was the result of communist manipulation, as he argued in relation to the docks strikes in 1949 for example. He also supported bans and proscriptions on communists from becoming either full-time or lay officials in the T&G in 1949.

This obsession had significant implications internationally, in addition. Deakin played a key role in undermining the WFTU, engineering a split in 1949 (see Chapter 3). As a result of this split the trade union movement became divided, internationally, reflecting the divisions of the Cold War more generally. There were implications for organising internationally, in parallel, as in the case of Gibraltar, for example, where an effective general secretary of the Gibraltar Confederation of Labour, Albert Fava, was deported for his communist connections.

Whatever his limitations however, Arthur Deakin did also have considerable achievements to his credit. He expanded the number of full-time officials in the T&G (building a machine over which he exercised maximum possible control). In addition, he built up the T&G's educational work, recognising the importance of having well-trained officials (even if his view of education was somewhat limited, as Chapter 5 explores in further detail).

The implications were crystal clear. We are all in this together. And it is you who are responsible for making any necessary sacrifices. Those who argue otherwise must be resisted. The national interest should be put first – a potentially powerful appeal with particular resonance in the aftermath of the Second World War and the election of Attlee's Labour government as Attlee went on to argue, emphasising the national interest still further in the context of the Cold War against communism:

We must not allow these subversive influences (by which he [i.e. Attlee] meant members of the Communist Party in the dock labour force) to wreck this tremendous social experiment which obliterated from the dockside the curse of casual labour and casual earnings.[8]

The history of labour disputes in the docks illustrates these tensions only too clearly.[9] As the Labour government became increasingly concerned to control wage rises, so the nationalised industries became the focus of attention. These industries were potentially more amenable to governmental pressure after all. And they might have been supposed to be amenable to more consensual approaches to industrial relations (via structures which included worker representation arrangements as in the National Dock Labour Corporation). Or were they? The reality seems to have been more complex.

The background to the 1948 dock strike related to the use of the National Dock Labour Scheme's disciplinary powers, disciplinary powers that have already been identified as a source of friction. Labour was supposed to have parity of representation with the employers, as it has already been outlined, with agreed mechanisms for resolving differences of view and avoiding disputes. But this was evidently not how these procedures were experienced among the rank and file. Some 30,000 dockers were affected by unofficial action in response to what was perceived as the National Dock Labour Board's arbitrary use of its disciplinary powers. As this unofficial action spread from London to Merseyside, the Labour government sent in troops and proclaimed a state of emergency.

Deakin was very critical of this type of unofficial action, as it has already been suggested. And he carried support for this position. At the biennial conference in Scarborough in 1949, for example, an emergency resolution was passed with an overwhelming majority, deeply deploring the continuation of an unofficial strike in London docks and calling on the members involved to resume normal work. 'It is their bounden duty to honour the obligations entered into by the Union on their behalf'.[10]

Reflecting on the 1949 dock strike in solidarity with Canadian seafarers, a strike that had spread across Avonmouth, Bristol, Leith, Newport, Southampton and the Royal and Surrey docks in London, Deakin was also clear about the nature of the underlying causes of such unofficial militancy. He argued that subversive elements had been at work, deliberately undermining the union and the Labour government that he so strongly supported. This was an argument that resonated in the context of the Cold War. In an article entitled 'Chaos Is Their Objective',

8 Quoted in Hennessy, *Having It So Good*, p.24–25.

9 Justin Davis Smith, *The Attlee and Churchill Administrations and Industrial Unrest, 1945–55* (Pinter, 1990).

10 MRC MSS.126/TG/1887/13. Record of the 13th Biennial Delegate Conference, 1949.

Figure 3: Striking dockers

Deakin quoted a Canadian seaman on 'the duplicity and diabolical plan of world communism to disrupt the industrial and economic life of this and other European countries during the year of 1949'. He argued that the Canadian seamen's strike had been undertaken at the secret request of the British Communist Party – to create an issue 'to involve the dockers in the Port of London'. Whether or not this had actually been the case has been questioned, with differing accounts from those directly involved. In Deakin's view though, rank-and-file militancy was to be explained by the malign influence of subversive elements – 'certain irresponsible people' who were 'trying to split the unity of the dockers by calling on our members to break away from the Transport and General Workers Union' he had already argued, back in 1946[11] – rather than by members' reactions to genuine grievances. He responded angrily to media suggestions that the union had lost touch with its members. This was grotesque, he argued.

Yet Deakin's approach did come in for criticism from frustrated dockers. This frustration was precisely what was demonstrated as the result of a subsequent dispute in the docks in 1954. Dockers in Hull became so frustrated with T&G that they decided to join another trade union, the National Amalgamated Stevedores & Dockers, the 'Blue' union – moves that were followed by dock workers in Liverpool as well. Overall some 10,000 dockers left the T&G in disgust at this time.

It is important to remember this background of rank-and-file frustration and unofficial action in the T&G during the Deakin years. This helps

11 Deakin, 'Union Policy on Wages', p.96.

Post-war Growth of Shop Stewards' Movement/Bans and Proscriptions

Southampton Docks

When the War started in 1939 and Southampton docks closed as a commercial port, dockers' leader Trevor Stallard moved to Coventry, first to the Daimler works where he was chairman of the shops stewards' committee and later to the Standard II works where he became convenor of shop stewards.

The aspect of Coventry that most impressed Trevor was the shop stewards' committees. In the docks at Southampton, the few shop stewards there never met as a committee and so, on his return to the docks in 1945 and subsequent election as shop steward, Trevor set up the first dockers' shop stewards' committee in the country. This was against Deakin's wishes, but the employers eventually recognised the committee which had the support of the young, up-and-coming official, Jack Jones.

By 1948/49 Trevor was on the district committee and General Executive Council (GEC) of the T&G. It was during this period that Deakin tried to expel Trevor because, when addressing a meeting of Liverpool dockers, Trevor told them which way the GEC members had voted over the acceptance of Stafford Cripps's pay policy.

When Communist Party members were proscribed from holding office in the T&G Trevor was removed from all committees, but the Southampton dockers refused to let Trevor and two other Party members, John Bonnin and Bill Taylor, be forced off the shop stewards' committee, to which end they were backed by the local officials. The port employers initially refused to recognise the committee with Communist Party members on it but, since the committee wouldn't meet them without Trevor and the others, they were forced to accept the situation. (Adrian Weir, 'Interview with Trevor Stallard', LSE trade union studies dissertation, 1981.)

to make sense of the massive turnaround that took place subsequently, when Frank Cousins became general secretary. As Cousins himself (with characteristic modesty) explained, 'I don't think I converted the feeling of the union when I became general secretary. All I did was to give expression to feelings that were there'.[12]

Deakin had not been able to have it all his own way when it came to controlling militancy in any case, despite the national policy framework. Communist Party members were indeed banned from holding key

12 Goodman, *The Awkward Warrior*, p.116.

positions in the T&G from 1949 onwards as part of his attempts to control militancy. But the enforcement of these controls proved more challenging in practice. There were activists who had their own ideas as the case of the Southampton dockers illustrates, for example, demonstrating the difficulties that Deakin encountered in practice when faced with determined resistance from the bottom up.

By the early to mid-fifties the whole context was changing in any case. The pressure on trade unions to moderate their members' demands was becoming increasingly unsustainable over time. Although there were trade union leaders who were still committed to 'responsible' trade unionism, this commitment began to shift still further under successive Conservative governments. The initial response to the re-election of a Tory government under Churchill's leadership in 1951 was somewhat muted, with Deakin setting a relatively co-operative tone. The TUC declared that it was 'our longstanding practice to seek amicably with whatever government is in power and through consultation jointly with Ministers and the other side of industry to find practical solutions to the social and economic problems facing the country'.[13]

By the end of the fifties, relationships were becoming decreasingly collaborative, however, with significant challenges. More of these later. But first, the parallels as well as the differences with the road haulage and passenger transport industries, further illustrations of the potential tensions between labour, capital and the state – even under a Labour government.

The Road Haulage and Passenger Transport Industries

The road haulage and passenger transport industries had their own histories of conflict in the post-war period too. There was a lorry drivers' strike in 1947, for instance, along with a London bus drivers' strike in 1949 (followed by further disputes in 1957 and 1958). So, what were such disputes about? And what might they illustrate about the relationships between labour, capital and the state, and the associated dilemmas for the trade union and labour movement over this period?

Long-distance lorry drivers' disputes provide case studies in point. There had already been a stoppage in 1946. Still frustrated by the lack of progress on wages and conditions, (including hours of work and holiday entitlements) after some nine months of talks, 30,000 long-distance lorry drivers came out on unofficial strike in 1947, focusing upon the demand for a 44-hour week. The strike threatened food supplies so the government sent in troops, only to provoke sympathy walk-outs as a result.

13 Quoted in Taylor, *The Trade Union Question*, p.84.

The drivers were determined to see their pay and conditions improve. And the Attlee government was determined to keep the economy moving in an increasingly difficult economic climate. On one occasion Deakin attempted to get the drivers back to work, addressing a mass meeting in the Memorial Hall, Farringdon Road, London to persuade them to do just that – only to be shouted down by the men in question. It was Frank Cousins who subsequently succeeded in persuading them to accept a deal; they were persuaded because they trusted him, apparently. It was said that Deakin never forgave Cousins for having succeeded where he himself had so signally – and so publicly – failed.

The passenger transport industry provides further illustrations of such tensions. Here too there were conflicts over the extent to which rank-and-file workers were to bear the costs of supporting a Labour government in power, with associated tensions with the T&G leadership. And there were questions about the nature – and the implications – of public ownership and planning more generally. Like the dock workers, the London busmen and tram workers had a radical history of struggles. They had also built up a strong rank-and-file movement in the pre-war period. Once the war was over there were similar pressures on them to co-operate with the newly elected Labour government, especially given the plans to nationalise transport. But what was this this actually to mean in practice?

There was an unofficial strike in London in 1947, even before the London Transport Executive was established under the British Transport Commission in 1948. As activist busmen described the situation themselves, there were continuing dissatisfactions over pay and conditions subsequently. London Transport's management structure was seen as a bureaucracy, rather than as a blueprint for organising services to the public or representing workers' interests, let alone offering a blueprint for socialist approaches to the management of public services. That wasn't part of the deal, it seemed. On the contrary, rank-and-file workers blamed this newly established structure for their deteriorating work conditions. This was not at all the outcome that workers had been anticipating in 1945. Back then, Bert Papworth, a key figure in the T&G, had celebrated the fact that the Labour Party and the trade unions were 'stronger than ever before', opening up the prospect of a country in which 'no child will go hungry, as many of us went hungry, no man be unable to find work, no people oppressed.[14] The hope was that public ownership was to be central to the development of such a socialist future. Or was it?

There had been gains in the 1944 agreement which had conceded the principle of the 44-hour maximum week. But this had included a flexibility clause under which a 46-hour could be scheduled as long as the average of 41 hours, 15 minutes was not exceeded. Sundays were only paid at

14   Albert Papworth, *A Busman Appeals to You* (Pamphlet MML, 1945), p.2.

time-and-a-quarter and there was no additional payment for Saturday afternoons. It was this that led to the 1947 unofficial strike in support of the demand for time-and-a-half for Sunday working. This was actually conceded the following year along with one day's paid leave for every Bank Holiday worked.

Then, in 1949, there was another unofficial strike. This time the issue was the demand for time-and-a-half for Saturday afternoons. The strike was lifted as a result of Deakin's intervention. But despite this, the demand was then conceded at arbitration. So whose side had the T&G leadership been on here?

The situation was very different by 1957, both in terms of government policies and in terms of the T&G's response under Frank Cousins's leadership. The Tory government had become increasingly determined to hold down wages in order to manage the problems of the British economy more generally – with public sector workers bearing the brunt with a 3 per cent ceiling on wage rises. The London Bus Section refused to accept this, putting in a claim for an almost 25 per cent increase instead. This was rejected by the London Transport Executive.

In January 1958 Sir Wilfred Neden, chief industrial commissioner at the Ministry of Labour, subsequently offered an inquiry, a proposal that a bus workers' conference decided to accept. Only Sir Wilfred's colleagues thought differently. Ian MacLeod, then Minister of Labour, rejected the proposal – which led to the bus workers voting for strike action, although with less than the required two thirds majority.

The dispute then went to arbitration. This resulted in the central bus staff being awarded an extra 8 shillings and sixpence, but the county services were awarded nothing – an outcome that merely provoked a further demand (for 10 shillings and sixpence). There was a massive majority this time (128 to 4) when this was put to the vote for strike action.

Frank Cousins didn't think that the busmen could succeed in taking on the Tory government, when the government intervened, overruling plans for conciliation – and he told them so. But Cousins, who believed in trade union democracy, still respected their decision to ignore his advice and come out on strike. He had supported the busmen who had come out in droves, 6,000 of them described as having come out willingly to a meeting at the Empress Hall to listen to his account of the facts that May – because they too trusted him.[15]

The busmen's solidarity over the seven weeks of this strike has been described as having been truly remarkable. It was the longest strike in the Section's history and one of the few London bus strikes to have been made official. 'By their determination they have at least placed a break on Government Policy which has sought to ensure that wages shall not rise

15 *The Record*, 1958, p.34.

Figure 4: Striking bus workers with Frank Cousins

with the cost of living', the *Record* argued at the time.[16] This was a fight for the whole of the trade union and labour movement, it was argued. But this was not quite how the dispute was seen by the leadership of the TUC. On the contrary, in fact.

Murray's history of the T&G also points to the secret support that was given to the Conservative government's position in relation to the bus workers' strike in 1958 – re-enforcing Potter's criticisms of the TUC leadership. These leaders took this position (albeit secretly) as a way of taking Cousins, the busmen's advocate, down a peg or two. They regarded Cousins as being too troublesome, Murray argues, because Cousins had made it very clear that he was not prepared to collude with putting the burden onto workers to solve Britain's economic problems.[17] This account was subsequently corroborated by one of those who had been centrally involved at the time, Ian MacLeod, the Conservative Minister of Labour.

The 1958 London bus strike lasted for seven weeks, representing a watershed, it has been argued, showing that governments couldn't continue to try to impose wage restraint without a struggle. Subsequent (Conservative) governments were prepared to take trade union activists on

16   *The Record*, 1958, p.32.
17   Murray, *The T&G Story*.

more aggressively in the years to come, however, raising wider questions about how to respond to these increasing pressures. The Labour Left criticised the TUC's leadership for not providing more support to workers in struggle. But the Labour Right blamed the busmen's strike, along with Cousin's support for it, for the Labour Party's subsequent electoral defeat, in 1959. Crosland and others argued that Labour policies needed to shift further to the Right in order for the Labour Party to become electable once again – arguments that have resurfaced on so many occasions subsequently. Frank Cousins himself explained that he had never believed that the most important thing was to elect a Labour government, however. 'The most important thing' he argued was 'to elect a Labour Government determined to carry out a socialist policy'.[18]

Struggles in the Motor Industry

Case studies from the motor industry illustrate different aspects of these changing relationships between labour, capital and the state. The firms in question were in the private sector, with less scope for governments to intervene directly as a result – although governments were certainly keenly interested in the sector's performance in this period, as the previous chapter has already outlined. The motor industry had been identified as a potential area of growth, in fact, key to increasing exports and so to offsetting Britain's balance of payments problems from 1947 onwards. This had been Stafford Cripps's vision, although he experienced disappointments here, as the previous chapter has also pointed out. On the contrary in fact. Boosted by Marshall Aid, Britain's competitors subsequently flourished.

By 1956 German car exports overtook British car exports, further emphasising the extent of the problems that needed to be faced. British production was insufficiently competitive, the result of years of inadequate investment. These failures were indicative of wider problems in British industry, demonstrating weaknesses that had been compounded by the devastations of war. Although the German economy had suffered even greater devastations, Germany – like a number of other Western European countries – benefited from investments via Marshall Aid, with the result that they were able to compete more effectively with Britain. So, what was to be done to improve productivity? And who was to bear the costs?

Matters came to a head in the motor industry in 1956 with the threat of 6,000 redundancies at the British Motor Corporation (BMC)'s plants at Longbridge, Birmingham and in Oxford. Workers were to be laid off – just like that – as part of management's attempts to increase productivity, getting more for less in other words. This dispute gained widespread

18 Goodman, *The Awkward Warrior*, p.324.

solidarity from T&G members in other sectors including the docks, thereby potentially paralysing production at the Longbridge plant. There was also mass picketing, one of the first – if not the very first – instances of this particular tactic.

The background to these disputes needs to be understood in the context of successful trade union organising in the Midlands in the post-war period. Jack Jones (the Coventry-based official who went on to become general secretary of the T&G in 1968) had been playing a key role here, actively promoting trade union organisation in the engineering industry in the region. This was sorely needed in this context. Jack Jones himself had anxieties about the risks of mass unemployment if the industry failed to adapt to the changing circumstances of post-war Britain.

During the war, order books had been full because production had focused on the war effort – production for the construction of aircraft, for example. But after the war the situation changed dramatically. Jack Jones wondered whether these years of assured order books were responsible for what he described as the lethargy which most employers were displaying when it came to the need to compete for orders to produce cars again. How were they going to be competitive in the post-war period when government orders came to an end? Vital skills could be lost to the engineering industry, via redundancies, if workers were to bear the brunt of employers' failures to meet these challenges, processes that had already been taking place before the BMC strike of 1956.

Redundancies were to be resisted for other reasons too. This was such a devastating experience. When workers were made redundant at this time, they had no formal rights to protect them. Employers did not have to make redundancy payments, nor did they have to negotiate procedures for deciding who to lay off. As Jack Jones put it himself: 'Compensation was unheard of: all we could do was mitigate the damage by slowing up the process and trying to ensure it was carried out as fairly as possible'.[19] Otherwise employers could simply decide to start with known militants to rid themselves of so-called 'trouble makers', further undermining resistance in the process. So, what was to be done?

When news of the 6,000 redundancies at BMC broke, Jack Jones realised that unless urgent action was taken, this would have destroyed trade union organisation at Longbridge (which was still relatively weakly organised anyway, with only 1,000 T&G members plus some members of other trade unions). He contacted the shop stewards to assure them of support. And he made media announcements explaining that the T&G would back strike action, urging BMC workers to oppose the redundancies and to demand the reinstatement of those discharged. BMC's actions were inhuman in his view and he said so with great force.

19 Jack Jones, *Union Man* (Collins, 1986), p.134.

Jack Jones
(1913–2009)

Like Frank Cousins before him, Jack Jones led the T&G in a progressive direction. He was the son of a Liverpool docker, working in the docks himself after losing a job as an apprentice engineer following the Wall Street crash of 1929. He joined the T&G, becoming a shop steward and then a delegate on the National Docks Group Committee.

After serving (and being wounded) in the Spanish Civil War, Jack Jones returned to Britain, becoming a full-time T&G official in Coventry before becoming regional secretary, playing a key role in organising in the motor industry. He was a committed socialist and an active supporter of the shop stewards' movement and industrial democracy. His role in organising the motor industry and resisting redundancies was a major feature of the T&G's history during this period.

Subsequently in 1968, Jack Jones went on to become general secretary of the T&G, leading the union on opposition to prices and incomes policies in the second half of the sixties. On retirement he went on to serve as president of the National Pensioners' Convention.

Most importantly, in 1956, Jack Jones was looking for support from a general secretary who shared his view, Frank Cousins, who readily agreed to support the strike financially. This was in marked contrast with the union's approach during the Deakin years. Jack Jones described Cousins's response to the request for support as 'the quickest response to such an approach in the history of the union' in fact.[20]

The first week of the strike was challenging. Not everyone responded to the strike call, so mass picketing was started in order to promote T&G appeals for solidarity. As Jack Jones himself explained, this tactic of mass picketing was almost unknown at the time although it became commonplace subsequently. It was a struggle to try to get support from road transport drivers, despite the appeals of the secretary of the Road Transport Group. But support was forthcoming from dockers in London and Liverpool and they were prepared to prevent the export of BMC cars. Still even so, in Jack Jones's view, this could have been a long and costly fight. In addition, the police were described as 'not helpful' – a mastery of understatement? – making picketing correspondingly more difficult.

20 Jones, *Union Man*, p.145.

Frank Cousins
(1904–1986)

Frank Cousins was the son of a Nottinghamshire miner. After spending five years in the mining industry he became a lorry driver, going on to become an official, and then national secretary of the T&G's Road Transport (Commercial) Group in 1948. He became assistant general secretary in 1955 and then general secretary in 1956. He was a member of the TUC's General Council between 1956 and 1969, and president of the International Transport Workers' Federation between 1958 to 1960 and then again between 1962 and 1964. He subsequently served in Harold Wilson's cabinet as Minister of Technology (1964–1966), resigning in protest against that government's freezing of incomes and prices.

Throughout his career, Frank Cousins supported progressive policies within the T&G, and then nationally as an MP and Minister of State in Harold Wilson's government. He was firmly committed to democracy within the union. And he was consistent in his support for socialist policies (subsequently opposing attempts to dilute them during Gaitskell's leadership of the Labour Party in the latter part of this period). Although he was not a communist himself, Frank Cousins was opposed to witch-hunts during the Bevin/Deakin years, looking to understand rank-and-file grievances rather than blaming unofficial stoppages on the machinations of 'reds under the bed'.

As a result, Frank Cousins was widely trusted by rank-and-file members. But TUC leaders were less convinced, viewing him as a troublesome Lefty, plotting against him on occasion as the history of the 1958 bus dispute illustrates, demonstrating widespread concerns about the progressive shift that the T&G was taking under his leadership. Frank Cousins himself was characteristically modest about his achievements, however, suggesting that he was only giving voice to views that were already widespread amongst the membership. 'It's not a Cousins union. It's a members' union', he explained (quoted in Margaret Stewart, *Frank Cousins* (Hutchinson, 1968), p.21).

BMC was probably aware of the union's limitations and challenges. But a breakthrough was achieved, all the same, even if this could not be described as 'winning hands down'. BMC agreed to withdraw some of the redundancies and to provide extra payments in some cases. They gave assurances that longer periods of notice would be given in any future redundancy situation and that negotiations would take place on compensation and the scope of future consultations. Given the lack of legal protection for workers in redundancy situations at this time, this marked a significant step forward. Reflecting on the outcome of the dispute, Frank Cousins pointed to these as significant, even if limited, achievements. 'We did at the end of the road establish a principle that on a national or company basis compensation for losing employment is something that can be discussed on behalf of manual workers', he argued, adding that if 'companies throw down the gauntlet' in such aggressive ways then 'reluctantly but nevertheless seriously, we will take them up'.[21]

Jack Jones had also described managers in the motor industry as being aggressive – 'notoriously bloody-minded'. But he still managed to negotiate further developments for the union in the aftermath of this strike. In fact, he persuaded management that it would actually be beneficial all round if shop stewards were to be treated more constructively rather than being driven underground by hostile management practices. As a result of these discussions management agreed for shop stewards to have paid time off for training. 'From little acorns big oaks grow', Jones concluded. From this first agreement 'grew the whole process of shop stewards training in works' time throughout the Midlands, and the whole country for that matter'.[22]

So how had all this been achieved? Trade union organisation had been relatively weak, even though this situation had been improving as a result of Jack Jones's efforts, backed by Frank Cousins's support, and by the threats posed by dockers' solidarity. How then had 'bloody-minded' managers been persuaded to make concessions that they were not legally obliged to make at this time? It might seem surprising that part of the answer seems to relate to the Conservative government of the day. Jack Jones's autobiography describes the help that the union received from a somewhat unlikely source – the Ministry of Labour. Officials working for the Minister, Ian MacLeod, had supported negotiations, whilst Ian MacLeod himself had told Parliament that he had been profoundly shocked by the overnight sackings. This, it should be remembered was the very same Ian MacLeod who was subsequently party to the secret negotiations with the TUC that undermined Frank Cousins's position in relation to the bus strike in 1958.

Part of the explanation for this apparent paradox could perhaps relate to wider changes in the climate of industrial relations over this period. Government attitudes were hardening in face of the increasingly evident difficulties of constraining inflation via voluntary agreements to limit wage increases. But this was not the only aspect to be considered. There could be other explanations too. More constructive, less combative industrial relations could be seen as desirable goals in their own right, from employers' points of view, potentially facilitating modernisation and industrial restructuring more effectively. Some of Britain's competitors

21 *The Record*, 1956, p.101.
22 Jones, *Union Man*, p.147.

were developing very different approaches to redundancies, for example, backed by compensation mechanisms that reduced workers' resistance to industrial change. This episode raises a series of questions in turn, questions about the role that capitalist states can play in promoting long-term capitalist interests more rationally – or not.

More of such questions later. Meanwhile, government interventions in the motor industry must have seemed extraordinary at the time, encouraging employers to listen to trade union demands on behalf of their workforces. This would have seemed especially surprising when contrasted with the role of T&G in the Deakin years, persuading workers to go back to work, seen by Deakin's critics as evidence that the trade union was on the employers' side rather than theirs.

The Print

Governments have had a history of intervening to strengthen the positions of workers in particularly vulnerable positions as with the introduction of the Dock Labour Scheme, as the previous section has already outlined. This had proved to be a mixed blessing in practice, however, bringing benefits when times were hard but proving more contentious in the context of full employment in the post-war period. Labour was supposed to have had parity of representation with the employers, with agreed mechanisms for resolving differences of view/disputes via the National Dock Labour Board. But in practice these structures were viewed as being biased towards the employers, leading to further conflicts as a result. How far would governments actually be prepared to go when it came to supporting workers in particularly vulnerable situations?

There would seem to be some parallels as well as differences here in relation to government interventions in different sections of the print and paper industries. These were complex industries, covering a wide variety of industrial sectors, from newspaper, magazine and book printing through to paper making, including the production of boxes and cartons. There were different types of employment across the sector, with strong craft sections as well as less skilled occupations in these industries – although the dividing lines between craft and non-craft work were shifting as technologies changed and new machines were introduced. In the post-war period, there were pressures on employers to do precisely this, in fact, in order to become more competitive (with increasing competition from the more cost-effective paper making industries of Canada and Sweden, for example).

Rates of pay varied too, with powerful pressures to protect the higher rates that craft workers had established, workers who were generally male (the struggle for equal pay for women will be explored more generally in Chapter 4). And there were different trade unions representing workers

Figure 5: Print workers striking for a 40-hour week

at different levels, in different sections of these industries, across various geographical locations. These different unions came together over time, forming the Graphical, Paper and Media Union (GPMU) merging with Amicus in 2004, before going on to merge with Unite in 2007.

Unsurprisingly there were widely varying interests to be represented in the post-war period though, from those who were most effectively organised to those who were far more vulnerable and so thought to be in need of state intervention to protect them. The story of state intervention in the box-making industry is a case in point. Before the First World War conditions in this industry have been described as terrible, especially amongst women homeworkers who were particularly hard to organise, given the fragmentation that was inherent in their work situations. Following the Trade Boards Act of 1909, a Box Industry Wages Council was set up in 1911, with the aim of improving the situation by establishing minimum wages rates with representation from workers, employers and independents who might have been expected to play a neutral role, ensuring fair play. But did they?

These structures were supposed to support the more vulnerable sections of the workforce. But this was not how they were actually experienced in practice. On the contrary, they were experienced as frustrating, constituting stumbling blocks to progress. This was especially the case since the so-called 'independents' – who were supposed to be independent – normally voted with the employers. From the early fifties, as a result, there were campaigns to get box making out of the wages council for the box industry.

The (Conservative) government of the day was unwilling to agree to abolish this wages council however – unless other alternative joint negotiating mechanisms were to be put in place. And the employers weren't easily persuaded, being happy with the wages council as it was, given that this typically came down on their side. So, the wages council remained in place, only to be finally abolished in 1974 (with effect from 1975). The implications would seem only too clear – governments could not be relied upon to support trade union rights. So, trade unionists needed to collaborate in solidarity across sectional differences. These were important pointers for the future, emphasising the case for finding ways forward beyond the demarcation disputes that had been a feature in these industries the past.

The Thomson strike clearly demonstrated the value of such solidarity in 1952. D.C. Thomson was a firm of printers and publishers based in Dundee, Glasgow, Manchester and London. The background to this dispute dates back to the 1926 General Strike and its aftermath, when the firm had decided to restart on a non-union basis (punishing trade union activists for their part in the General Strike). New employees had been required to sign a document agreeing not to be a trade union member. Unsurprisingly this had been contentious. Varying approaches had been made to Thomson's since then, attempting to negotiate trade union recognition. Meanwhile the unions, including the National Society of Operative Printers and Assistants (NATSOPA) and the National Union of Printing, Bookbinding and Paper Workers (NUPBW) had been busy recruiting members.

The events of 1952 were sparked off when Thomson's sacked 15 men in Manchester, at least ten of whom were members of the Paper Workers Union, following this up by sacking a NATSOPA member – and Father of the Chapel, i.e. shop steward – in Glasgow. As a result, NATSOPA and NUPBW came together in support of industrial action, successfully appealing to other trade unions for support – both financial and industrial – in their turn. This included support from T&G members who refused to drive lorries taking paper supplies to Thomson's.

This level of solidarity proved crucial. There was profound appreciation for the support provided by NATSOPA, the TUC, the Scottish TUC and these other trade unionists acting in solidarity against this anti-union attack, re-affirming their determination to intensify the fight until the 'infamous document denying the right of their workers to join a trade union is withdrawn'.[23]

Meanwhile questions were being asked in Parliament, the Minister

---

23 James Moran, *NATSOPA* (Oxford University Press, 1964), p.126.

of Labour was brought into the dispute and legal proceedings were set in motion. Thomson's were concerned that the trade unions were determined to have closed shops, which would have been unacceptable in their view. But the reality was, it has been argued, that the trade unions in question were being far more statesmanlike. They were prepared to agree that they were only seeking the right to join a trade union – workers could make up their own minds as to whether they became union members – or not. It was argued that this could have provided the basis for a settlement, but only if the dismissed men were also reinstated, which they weren't. There were further discussions in Parliament and meetings between the TUC and the then prime minister, Winston Churchill. But the matter dragged on until 1953, by which time most of the Glasgow men had found new jobs anyway.

Some gains had indeed been made. But the men who had been dismissed had not been reinstated. There was no resolution by 1953 when the dispute was finally suspended. Hardly a massive victory then? Still the dispute was significant for all that. In addition to the gains in relation to trade union recognition there were gains for the longer term, it would seem, gains in terms of building solidarity across the paper and print industries and beyond, in the wider trade union and labour movement, including the T&G. This was centrally important, demonstrating the possibility of proactive responses to increasing pressures from employers in this period and subsequently, building trade union solidarity, across sectoral divides.

Further Disputes

Solidarity was also centrally important in the struggles that took place subsequently, in 1958–1959. The state has been seen as having been more directly involved here, as the historian of NATSOPA has also explained, arguing that '[t]he major dispute in 1959 was not of a straight-forward industrial nature. Union leaders believed that it had strong political overtones and that the Conservative government, seeking to force wage restraint on the country, had chosen the printing industry for a show-down'.[24]

The dispute itself was about both wages and conditions, with a six weeks' strike in support of the demand for a 10 per cent wage increase and the demand for a 40-hour week. This was a massive stoppage with 120,000 workers on strike. Four thousand firms were affected, covering the general print and 1,000 local newspaper offices. Here was a case of solidarity across different print industries on a ground-breaking scale, with manual workers taking action together in pursuit of their common interests.

24 Moran, *NATSOPA*, p.136.

The Minister of Labour eventually intervened, with an independent chair brought into the process to bring the dispute to a resolution. The workers voted to return to work, on the basis of a settlement which was to be finalised with implementation phased in over time, the balance of the 10 per cent wage increase being eventually finalised in 1962. The 40-hour week took time too, implementation eventually being completed in 1962. Importantly too, it was agreed that if new techniques or methods of production were to be introduced, consideration would be given to preventing, or at least alleviating unemployment, including via retraining, shorter hours or additional holidays. And there were improvements to the relative position of women in the industry, although much remained to be achieved in this respect (see Chapter 4 on struggles for equalities, including struggles within the print industry).

This brings the argument to the implications of the 1959 strike more widely. The outcome gave a boost to union activity and confidence. It was not just that the trade unions were anticipating ways of responding to industrial restructuring – although they were indeed doing precisely that. It was also that there had been a united approach by nine print unions, negotiating across the craft/non-craft divide, with solidarity from the trade union and labour movement more generally. Most importantly too, this had been a nationwide strike, bringing trade unionists together across different areas and regions, with different employers involved. The trade union and labour movement was responding to the challenges of industrial change more strategically, taking initiatives proactively, aiming to build solidarity across previous divides rather than simply reacting to increasing pressures from employers, backed by an increasingly determined Conservative government. As the history of NATSOPA concludes: 'Union members probably realize that they cannot continue in watertight compartments' in challenging times,[25] even if these challenges were difficult to address in practice.

There were potentially wider lessons here, pointing to the relevant trades unions' attitudes to change, looking forward to a modernised industry without artificial barriers with no room for 'curious caste divisions based on the past'.[26] Trade unions were recognising the need to develop their own strategies for change, building solidarity, based on more effective structures, for the future. There would seem to be powerful parallels with potentially wider implications here.

25 Moran, *NATSOPA*, p.151.
26 Moran, *NATSOPA*, p.153.

Memories of the 1959 Print Dispute

Ted Chard, a retired, elected national official of Society of Graphical and Allied Trades (SOGAT) and then GPMU, recalled his own experiences of the 1959 strike. Like so many in the print industry, Ted came from a family with a proud tradition of trade union membership. As an apprentice he was not actually on strike himself, but support for the strike was absolutely solid throughout the workforce and the apprentices at Cornwall Press, in Stamford Street, London, which was where he worked at the time. The entire membership of the nine print unions involved was mobilised with solidarity action across the UK and France (to stop the movement of paper and ink).

Ted explained that although the apprentices were not on strike themselves, they were absolutely determined that they would refuse to carry out any tasks that related to production. One day a manager came down to see the apprentices, carrying a package. He explained that this package needed to be delivered to Fleet Street that afternoon. He lined up the apprentices and asked the first one if he would deliver the package. The apprentice looked him straight in the eye and refused. The manager went to the next apprentice and asked him the same question, only to receive the same answer. He went on down the line. No one blinked. Not a single apprentice agreed to take the package.

At this point, the manager began to lose his temper, shouting that he would tear up the indenture papers of anyone who refused to deliver the package. Still no one budged. Eventually he was forced to retreat, recognising that the apprentices had worsted him with their solidarity.

Reflecting on the significance of the 1959 strike, Ted emphasised the importance of this culture of solidarity in the print industry which had been 100 per cent organised at the time. There were strong family traditions; maybe 90 per cent of the workforce had family members in the trade. The 1959 strike had been an enlightening experience showing what this kind of solidarity could achieve. No on wavered. No one weakened. They were all in it together with an enormous sense of pride in the union. There were parallels here with the traditions of solidarity in the mines and docks.

John Johnson had similar reflections to share, drawing on his experiences as an apprentice at the Amalgamated Press in Southwark, London, during the 1959 strike. He began by describing the working conditions which were horrendous, a cauldron of noise and dust; health and safety arrangements were virtually nil with guillotines that were death traps. But the dispute itself had been about hours of work, low pay and holiday entitlements.

Here too at Amalgamated Press the strike had been absolutely solid. The picket line had been completely peaceful, with one lonely policeman on duty there, cordial and talkative with the strikers. The chapel meetings had been packed. And the community had been completely behind the strikers. There were some instances when families put pressure behind the scenes, because of the financial hardships that were being experienced. But no one would say this publicly. This was about solidarity across communities as well as solidarity across workplaces. Both John and Ted drew contrasts between the strength of solidarity at that time, and the ways in which the print industry had been decimated with such violence, in subsequent years.

These views were affirmed through discussions with three women who all went on to play leading roles in the print industry subsequently, Marie Bucksey (nee Thompson), Carol Garner and Ivy Smith. Ivy had been jobbing at the time, having left her job at Amalgamated Press when she got married (which was normal at that time). At the time of the strike she was working three days a week at a firm in Bowling Green Lane, together with two casual shifts on the other days (via the 'House', the system that was organised by the print unions to allocate jobs fairly).There wasn't always casual work available though. Ivy did get strike pay, but it wasn't easy for people, financially.

Ivy didn't have children yet. But her husband (who also worked in the print industry) was on strike too – although he also had strike pay and got some work on national newspapers. There was an irony here. Ivy remembered going on a march to Fleet Street to ask for support, to persuade the unions on the national newspapers to come out on strike in support. They didn't which was disappointing. But on the other hand, they were paying into the strike fund. And casual jobs on the national newspapers were keeping some families going during the strike.

These leading women trade unionists also emphasised that the 1959 strike was absolutely solid. This included the apprentices although they were still formally working. But they had effectively nothing to do because of the strike. Doing nothing was very boring actually, as Marie explained!

Some people were put under pressure from family members who were trying to persuade them to go back to work though. Although she was not on strike herself because she was an apprentice, Marie was aware of the tragic effects that financial pressures could have in some cases, even leading to a suicide. Whatever the pressures inside the home though, anti-strike views were not expressed in public (as John had already explained). On the contrary. As a result, this solidarity paid off. And employers were picked off, one by one.

Although the 40-hour week was only implemented in 1962, much was achieved as a result. The trade unions gained strength and confidence, realising that 'there were things we could do'. 'From little victories we gained strength' (Interview with Marie Bucksey, conducted by the author, 29 July, 2020). This was the case for the women too, not just the men.

Ivy explained that these achievements also needed to be understood in relation to the wider context and the mood of the times. People were confident. The mood was 'on the up' and this was true of the women as well as the men. This confidence lasted throughout that period and beyond, right up to the end of the seventies, when jobs were beginning to disappear as the result of industrial restructuring, with firms moving out of London, shedding jobs in the process. And then came the Thatcher government with its attacks on the trade union movement and anti-trade union legislation. By the time of the Wapping dispute the situation was really changing, undermining trade union strengths. But these are issues to be explored further in the following volume.

Conclusions

This chapter started from the dilemmas that the trade union and labour movement faced under Attlee's reforming Labour government in the post-war period. Trade union leaders, such as the T&G's Arthur Deakin, were prepared to make very considerable concessions, it has been argued, despite significant reservations about any form of governmental interference in free collective bargaining mechanisms. Pressures grew from the very start however, as the economy struggled – especially given the impact of international factors. Summarising the achievements and lessons of the period from 1945 onwards, from the standpoint of 1960, Palme Dutt wrote as follows:

> The Attlee-Bevin leadership proceeded to embark on a programme of vicious anti-Soviet hostility from the outset, the cold war, surrender of Britain to the United States, construction of the atom bomb, American bomber bases in Britain, colonial wars, N.A.T.O., the rebuilding of German militarism and colossal rearmament. When the bill for all this resulted in austerity, the reversal of social reforms and the wage freeze, the previous mass enthusiasm gave place to mass disillusionment. On this basis, not through their own virtues, the previously discredited Tories were able to creep back.[27]

Whether or not such an indictment can be fully justified is another question. But the links between Britain's domestic and foreign policies do seem to constitute a key element in the story of these times. Under such pressures, post-war Labour governments found themselves faced with increasing dilemmas. And so did trade union leaders – questioned as to whose side they were on when push came to shove. Governmental pressures for wage restraint were soon being accompanied by conflicting pressures – from their own rank and files. T&G general secretaries took sharply contrasting positions when faced with such pressures – although

27 Quoted in Allen Hutt, *British Trade Unionism* (Lawrence & Wishart, 1975), pp.214–215.

there were trade union leaders who continued to take more equivocal positions, even under succeeding Conservative governments. Particular trade union leaders' willingness to engage in a secret plot to undermine Frank Cousins's position on the 1958 bus strike makes this point only too clearly.

Conservative government interventions were not all negative in any case, even if the results of their interventions tended to favour the employers' side as a general rule. But there were cases where governments were seen to be supporting workers, even if such examples involved the promotion of industrial modernisation for the longer term. This would seem to have been the case in relation to redundancies in the motor industry, for example. Ironically it was the employers who seemed to be the problem in many cases, accused of failing to invest to modernise British industry, lagging behind Britain's competitors internationally as a result.

There were examples of more positive responses from trade unions, however, addressing previous divisions within their ranks as the previous section has also illustrated. Subsequent volumes explore the implications of such changes in trade union structures and approaches more fully, including the potential implications for equalities agendas. But first, the following chapter explores the international context and its implications in further detail, with a focus on policy changes within the T&G and their wider impact.

Before moving on to the next chapter though, you might like to reflect on the following questions for yourself.

Questions for Discussion: Chapter 2

- How far do you agree with Palme Dutt's conclusions about the reasons for the return of a Tory government in 1951? (You might want to revisit this question after reading the next chapter too, to see if this has affected your view in any way).

- What else – if anything – could the Attlee government have done to resolve Britain's economic and industrial relations problems?

- What else – if anything – might trade union leaders have done, in face of the dilemmas of the immediate post-war period?

- What about rank-and-file activists? What else – if anything – might they have done? Or should they have done?

- How far did relationships between capital, labour and the state change – or not change – between 1945 and 1960?

- What – if any – fundamental differences were there in the relationships between capital, labour and the state across the public sector and the private sector over this period?

- How would you apportion responsibility for the Labour Party's electoral defeats in the 1950s, including its defeat in 1959?

- What, if any, parallels would you draw between debates on the outcome of the 1959 election and more contemporary debates on electoral defeats?

3

International Solidarity – or Not?

'The general assumption was that we were still a great power and were going to be one again' reflected a historian, turned colonial office official, going on to point out that he himself hadn't believed this, even at the time, at the end of the Second World War.[1] Britain's position in the world had in fact been seriously contested, as previous chapters have already suggested. Jean Monnet (a key mover in the development of moves towards European integration) put the position more sharply still. It was his view that, unlike France and Germany, where there were only too vivid memories of defeat and occupation, Britain felt 'no need to exorcise history'. It was, he argued, the price of victory – 'the illusion that you could maintain what you had without change'.[2]

Britain's international position was most certainly changing however, whether colonial officials were prepared to recognise the fact or not. With Indian independence, Britain embarked on a process of decolonisation, a process that began to gather momentum by the end of the fifties. But the notion that Britain should continue to be acknowledged as a great power has persisted, with claims to a 'seat at the top table' – a notion with continuing implications for contemporary times, both at home and abroad.

Meanwhile the international context was changing dramatically. Wartime alliances with the Soviet Union began to splinter apart soon after the end of the Second World War. This was followed by rapidly growing threats to peace – or fears of threats to peace – with the so-called 'Cold War'. Defence spending impacted on domestic spending as a result, with increasing pressure from Britain's decision to develop its own nuclear weapons (although nuclear weapons were actually advocated by some politicians as being cheaper than having so many troops on the ground,

---

1 Quoted in Hennessy, *Never Again*, p.224.
2 Quoted in Hennessy, *Never Again*, p.392.

the residue of Britain's past when 'the sun never set on the British Empire', from East to West across the globe).

This chapter sets out to explore the impact of these changes in the international context, as they related to the trade union and labour movement in general and to the T&G more specifically. The previous chapter has already raised questions about the impact of Britain's changing international role on economic development and job opportunities back in Britain, along with the impact on public expenditure more generally during this period. But how did the Cold War impact in terms of the development of international solidarity, or not? And how were trade unionists affected by threats to world peace? There were those who suggested that these threats were not an issue for trade unions per se in any case. But others took a very different view. When challenged about the relevance of CND, Frank Cousins explained that when faced with the risk of what he termed 'mass suicide', peace was most certainly an issue for us all. The T&G played a leading role throughout this period but in extremely different ways, shifting direction very significantly from the mid-fifties onwards.

The chapter starts from Britain's changing role in the immediate post-war period in the context of the emergence of the Cold War, Marshall Aid and NATO. Following in Bevin's footsteps, T&G's Arthur Deakin was a key player, both in Britain itself and in the trade union movement internationally. The chapter then moves on to focus on the great powers' competition to acquire nuclear weapons, with Arthur Deakin's successor, Frank Cousins, playing a very different role in support of peace and disarmament, despite Britain's attempts to compete in the nuclear arms race in order to maintain its 'seat at the top table'.

Britain's Changing Role in a Rapidly Changing World

Peter Hennessy's history of Britain in the fifties starts with some insightful reflections on Britain's changing role in the world along with Britain's widespread reluctance to recognise – and accept – these new realities. He quotes the historian Peter Laslett's contemporary comment that

> [o]ne of the difficulties of being an Englishman in 1950 is the persistent delusion that it is after the deluge. It is not. The deluge is still with us [...]. Britain has commitments far greater than she could possibly fulfil [...]. Insistence on its traditional rights by a power in decline leads perilously quickly to war [...]. The peace of the world depends therefore on the Englishman being able to reconcile himself to a continuous diminution in the consequence of his country.[3]

---

3 Hennessy, *Never Again*, pp.1–2.

(Note the emphasis on the 'Englishman', suggesting a context in which decision-making was still seen to be dominated by men from the imperial heartlands?)

These debates run throughout this period. From being a leading, if not the leading imperial power, Britain faced tough choices about the future of its colonies. There was widespread resistance to decolonisation, although this was the necessity that had to be faced, right from the start, with Clement Attlee's recognition of the case for Indian independence in 1947 (with powers transferred in 1948). His foreign secretary, T&G's former general secretary Ernest Bevin, was generally supportive of Britain's international commitments too, including the British Mandate in Palestine. He too though (if reluctantly) came to accept the specific case for abandoning Britain's direct involvement following the loss of some 100 British lives in the bombing of the King David Hotel in Jerusalem by the Irgun group of Zionists in 1946. The potential costs (including the human costs) of staying put were only too obvious. These decisions were deeply contentious though, reflecting wider divisions within governments as well as between them. Bevin himself believed that these challenges were temporary difficulties that could be overcome in time as Britain recovered from the after-effects of war. He was not alone in such optimism, even if this was far from being universally shared at the time.

After Labour's election defeat in 1951, the Conservative governments that followed took varying positions on Britain's imperial role as well. There were those who were deeply resistant to decolonisation. But others took a different (more realistic) view, although this was extremely contentious at the time. When Harold Macmillan, the Conservative prime minister who succeeded Winston Churchill after the brief premiership of Anthony Eden, commissioned a report on the practical costs and benefits of Empire, country by country, this was to be confidential. Too controversial to be considered at all? Such was the opposition that he was anticipating from within his own ranks when faced with such a pragmatic approach to the Empire's future.

Meanwhile, Britain was not just facing challenging decisions about the future of its Empire. Britain's declining powers were becoming increasingly apparent, more generally, in the context of shifting power balances on the international scene following the Second World War. Wartime alliances were so soon to fall apart, as it has already been suggested, with the emergence of the Cold War between the two great powers and their allies, the USA on the one hand and the USSR on the other. So where was this to leave Britain? And how should trade unions engage with this emerging scenario?

The predominant view was that Britain could and should continue to play a key role, with a 'seat at the top table', leading the Commonwealth of Nations that was to begin to take its place besides what remained of Britain's Empire, alongside its relationships with Western Europe (relationships that the US was generally keen to encourage at this period). In such ways Britain would be the USA's key ally in the Cold War, safeguarding its international significance by developing its own nuclear deterrents. This had been Winston Churchill's vision, a vision that had been widely, although by no means generally, accepted.

Bevin was a powerful proponent of such an approach as well, having already been quoted as arguing the case for a British bomb with a bloody great Union Jack on it. As foreign secretary he was described as working 'to harness the trade union [i.e. T&G] by and large to a Churchillian foreign policy [...] pro-American, anti-Soviet and actively hostile to the new popular movements that were everywhere arising against the bankrupt old order'.[4] Such views were shared by a number of leading trade unionists at the time, including Bevin's successor as T&G general secretary, Arthur Deakin.

The notion that Britain could play such a strong independent role was challenging to maintain however, as the debacle of the Suez affair in 1956 so clearly illustrated (when Britain and France sent a military expedition to 'protect' the Suez Canal, only to find themselves forced to retreat, due to the lack of US backing). So what did Britain's independent role on the world stage actually mean, when push came to shove? To what extent was Britain actually dependent on the US in practice? Was the US a reliable ally in any case? And how did this all relate to the Cold War itself, and Western powers' fears of the USSR as these fears played out both at home and abroad?

The Trade Union and Labour Movement in the Context of the Cold War

Trade unions contained their own differences of perspective when it came to support for movements for colonial freedom, just as it has had differences on international policies, peace and disarmament more generally. The quotation from Palme Dutt that figured in the final section of the previous chapter illustrates a particular, if contentious, alternative to mainstream views on Britain's approach. The story of the development – and subsequent undermining – of the WFTU provides a case study in point, demonstrating precisely such differences as they played out in practice.

The WFTU was the first real attempt to build an all-inclusive federation of national federations from every continent, cutting across differences of political orientation. During the Second World War, British and Soviet trade unions had co-operated with each other, international forms of

---

4 Murray, *The T&G Story*, p.98.

co-operation that were to be taken forward afterwards with a conference in London in 1945, chaired by Walter Citrine of the TUC. This provided the groundwork for the launch of the WFTU in Paris later that year. This was an anti-fascist trade union alliance. The aims were to protect workers' rights, with full employment, a 40-hour week, social insurance and trade union participation in economic life – pretty standard trade union aims, in fact. And for the first four years, this was indeed the focus of WFTU activities, supporting workers' rights, including workers' rights in the context of struggles for colonial freedom. By 1947 there were 71 affiliated national trade union centres, representing some 70 million workers worldwide.

There were areas of contention all the same, even before the onset of the Cold War. For example, the TUC's Walter Citrine hadn't wanted to discuss Indian independence, the precursor of subsequent differences of attitude towards struggles for colonial freedom, just as the Dutch didn't want to discuss independence for Indonesia. Even so however, the WFTU did take stands on workers' rights in colonial contexts, with a pamphlet on 'Discrimination Against Coloured People', for instance. This pamphlet challenged differential pay rates in countries such as Kenya, Tanganyika, South Africa, Australia, the Belgian Congo and Indonesia, for example, along with differences in conditions of work and social insurance provision, restrictions on movement and the lack of trade union rights.[5] Colonial exploitation was an essential feature of imperialism, this pamphlet concluded, referring to the WFTU's Second Congress resolution on the importance of developing trade unions in the colonies as key to the way forward internationally.

The US trade union organisations had been hesitant about the formation of WFTU, however, with growing fears about the USSR's expanding influence. These differences sharpened as the Cold War gathered momentum from 1947, with the extension of communist governments in Eastern and Central Europe and the USSR's blockade of Berlin in retaliation for the Western powers' actions in West Germany. The politics of fear were escalating on both sides, the East fearing that the US-backed Marshall Plan was aimed at extending US influence in Europe; and the West fearing Soviet advances in the opposite direction. With the benefit of hindsight it seems that both sides probably overestimated the extent of the likelihood of such threats in practice. (It seems that Stalin distrusted Burgess and Maclean, the British spies who had defected to the USSR, suspecting that they were double agents sent to lure him into a false sense of security when they played down the realistic chances of the British committing such acts of aggression). But the fears themselves were widespread enough, leading to increasing tensions and the further development of nuclear weapons, tensions that dominated the politics of the Cold War period.

5   Mary Yeates, *Discrimination Against Colonial People* (WFTU Publication, undated).

Deakin's Involvement with the WFTU

The WFTU was an early victim of this rapidly shifting post-war scene. When Walter Citrine resigned as WFTU president he was succeeded by Arthur Deakin from the T&G in 1946. Although – like Citrine – Deakin had seemed initially supportive, differences were soon to emerge. By 1948 Arthur Deakin was telling the TUC that 'the WFTU is rapidly becoming nothing more than a platform and instrument for the furthering of Soviet policy'[6] – a view that it has been argued didn't stand up to further examination of the facts. Still the TUC did subsequently critique the WFTU's support for 'economically backward peoples, and, in particular the colonial peoples to rise in revolt against the Western democracies, in order to embarrass the latter, and to facilitate the propagation of Communism'[7] (i.e. support for movements for colonial freedom was to be equated with support for communism?)

The British Foreign Office became convinced of the case for bridling (i.e. controlling) and eventually undermining the WFTU.[8] But there were anxieties about the potential fall-out from being seen to promote such a divisive policy. So the discussions with Deakin and the TUC that followed were conducted in secret. It seems that Deakin was in regular clandestine discussions in fact, including discussions with Bevin, as foreign secretary, throughout this period, leading up to the split with the WFTU in 1949.

It was the Marshall Plan that provided the spark. This was a highly contentious issue, supported by those in favour of this US intervention in Europe but increasingly opposed by those who came to fear that the Marshall Plan would undermine progressive positions, opening the way for austerity programmes to promote profitability at workers' expense. At the beginning of 1948 the TUC demanded that the WFTU's Executive Bureau should discuss the Marshall Plan, a demand that was therefore resisted. The WFTU's Executive Board's counter proposal was that this should be a matter for the next full Executive Committee to consider. But the TUC went ahead with calling a separate European conference, backed by the US trade union organisations.

Relations continued to deteriorate, with further demands on the WFTU, leading up to an ultimatum from the TUC that the WFTU should suspend all its activities for a year whilst a small committee would examine whether there was a future for the organisation. Otherwise the TUC would leave – supported by the US Congress of Industrial Organizations (CIO).

---

6 Tom Sibley, *Anti-communism: studies of its impact on the UK labour movement in the early years* (1945–1950) of the Cold War (PhD thesis, University of Keele, 2008), p.214.

7 Sibley, *Anti-communism*, p.214.

8 Anthony Carew, *Labour under the Marshall Plan* (Manchester University Press, 1987).

This has been described as the TUC and the CIO playing political games here, making demands that no self-respecting organisation would accept without debate and approval by its highest body, the WFTU's World Congress. The TUC's suspension proposal was seen as unconstitutional.

Still the CIO and the TUC persisted along this path (taking account of pressures from their respective governments). This was despite the fact that neither organisation had the approval of a delegate conference to provide democratic legitimacy for taking such a position forward. But they were not to be deterred. When it became clear that they were in a minority, Deakin proceeded to walk out, along with the Carey (from the CIO) and Kuypers (from the Nederlandse Vuurtoren Vereniging [NVV], Holland).

The WFTU was signally undermined as a result of this walkout, engineered by Deakin and others in 1949. It subsequently continued as a much more limited organisation. Meanwhile Western trade union federations formed the International Confederation of Free Trade Unions (ICFTU) with the backing of the US, thereby reinforcing Cold War differences internationally.

The issue continued to be contentious within the T&G however. Although the majority supported Deakin's position, there was a minority that continued to advocate reaffiliating to the WFTU. At the biennial conference in Southsea in 1953, for example, a motion was put forward calling for re-affiliation –although this was lost. The issue re-emerged subsequently at the biennial conference in Torquay in 1957, with a motion calling on the TUC to negotiate rebuilding links with WFTU, but once again this was also lost, despite the wider shifts in the T&G's political leadership since the election of Frank Cousins as general secretary.

Deakin's Involvement with Gibraltar

Deakin played a key role in Gibraltar more specifically too, an issue with even more direct implications for the T&G which had been recruiting there (if not entirely successfully) since well before the Second World War. Gibraltar was a British colony, seen as vitally important as a naval base. The Ministry of Defence was a major employer, with English, Gibraltarian and Spanish workers, including T&G members as well as members of the Gibraltar Congress of Labour (GCL). This (GCL) had been formed in 1947, at least partly, if not entirely, due to workers' frustration with the T&G's approach to organising/failing to organise effectively during that period. The GCL soon grew to some 2,500 members, mostly in the dockyards and other public sector bodies.

Relationships between GCL and the T&G have been described as somewhat fraught, (unsurprisingly perhaps in the circumstances) mirroring the potential tensions that were seen to exist between GCL and the then Labour government. This was because the Foreign Office was

Figure 6: Arthur Deakin

concerned to hold back calls for self-determination for Gibraltar given its strategic position as a naval base. And conversely the GCL was seen to be associated with campaigns for political rights as well as workplace rights through its links with the Association for the Advancement of Civil Rights (AACR), an organisation that was working for civil rights, potentially leading to political independence for the future. Hence some of these tensions between them and the T&G.

In the event the GCL ended up by affiliating to the ICFTU. The T&G became the main trade union in the area, and the status of Gibraltar continued to be contested, remaining to be the subject of further negotiations as part of the process of Britain leaving the European Union. But this is to leap way too far ahead. Back then, the question for Deakin and others remained how to manage these threats from the GCL. Which is where the GCL's general secretary, Albert Fava, comes into the story.

Albert Fava had been born in Gibraltar in 1912. He became an activist, supporting the Republican side against Franco in the Spanish

Civil War before ending up taking refuge in Britain, along with many others from Gibraltar, during the Second World War. Albert Fava joined the Communist Party there, gaining a reputation as a very effective organiser, which was the reason for his recruitment to the GCL in 1948. As general secretary he was very successful, it seems, both as an organiser and as an experienced leader, moving GCL strategically forwards in a progressive direction, hence the moves against him that followed. It was only months before Albert Fava was to be deported back to Britain on what seemed to be highly spurious allegations of subversive activities at the time.

Albert Fava's deportation was certainly contentious. A petition in support of his case was signed by nearly 5,000 people. Questions were asked in Parliament. And the National Council for Civil Liberties (NCCL, now 'Liberty') took up his case. There seemed to be a conspicuous lack of evidence about his alleged subversive activities, a lack of evidence that remained even when secret files were opened up many years later. The evidence simply wasn't there. But Albert Fava lost his appeal. He stayed in Britain subsequently, actively working for trade unions for the rest of his life. He died in 1993.

To Summarise the Argument So Far

From the end of the Second World War through to the emergence of the Cold War, the T&G was absolutely central to the history of trade unionism on an international scale. Bevin and Deakin were both pivotal figures, with major impacts, supporting a Churchillian approach to decolonisation, along with a Churchillian approach to the case for supporting the US rather than the USSR during this period. There were negative effects in terms of the promotion of trade union rights and national liberation struggles as a result, just as there had been negative effects in terms of the promotion of bans and proscriptions on communists, and increasing expenditures on defence rather than expenditures on industrial investment and public services back home in Britain. 'Reds under the bed' were blamed when trade unions mobilised abroad, as in the case of the GCL in Gibraltar, just as they had been blamed in Britain too – rather than trade union militancy being understood in terms of resistance in the face of legitimate grievances. Meanwhile nuclear weapons were being developed further in response to the Cold War, dominated by mutual fears on either side of the 'Iron Curtain'. But all this was to change in the latter part of the 1950s.

Frank Cousins, Movements for Colonial Freedom, Peace and Nuclear Disarmament

The T&G's approach changed dramatically when Frank Cousins became general secretary in 1956. This marked the beginning of a very different era for the union. Frank Cousins has been described as dragging the union from the darkness to the light. His biographer, Geoffrey Goodman, summarised his greatest contribution as having been 'to transform his own union from a passive and perhaps even docile giant to a potential driving force' for democratic change.[9] But these new directions were not entirely without precedents. There had been opposition to the Cold War policies that had been pursued by Bevin and Deakin in the immediate post-war period, just as there had been opposition to their approaches towards wage restraint at home under the Attlee governments, as the previous chapter has already outlined. Frank Cousins himself was well aware of the existence of pressures for change within the T&G, even before he himself took office. He has already been quoted on this. By no means a communist himself, Frank Cousins has been described as being resistant to Cold War witch-hunts within the trade union movement. He was far more supportive of movements for peace and international solidarity.

There had been parallel pressures from within the Labour Party itself, where there were those who were committed to peace and internationalism, during the Attlee governments. Nye Bevan had resigned in protest at the imposition of health charges, levied in order to pay for defence expenditure in the context of the Korean War as previous chapters have already pointed out. Bevan had been far from gung-ho about the Cold War. And although critical of Stalin, he was doubtful as to whether the USSR was actually planning acts of military aggression, let alone planning a wholescale invasion of Western Europe. Attlee himself seems to have doubted this too, despite his antipathy to communism in general and his suspicions that communist agitators were behind so many outbreaks of industrial unrest back in Britain.

Like Frank Cousins, the Labour Left had also supported mobilisations for colonial freedom. Outstanding figures had included Fenner Brockway, MP, who was the first chair of the Movement for Colonial Freedom (MCF) founded in 1954 (subsequently renamed 'Liberation'), a movement that was supported by 70 MPs including Harold Wilson, Barbara Castle and Tony Benn, as well as having support from other celebrities such as the composer, Benjamin Britten. Most importantly the MCF had widespread support amongst the trade union and labour movement, promoting solidarity with trade union and national liberation activists in a range of contexts internationally. The MCF campaigned against colonial

---

9 Geoffrey Goodman, *Brother Frank* (Panther, 1969).

authorities' restrictions on trade union activities in the colonies, from the internment, and in some cases banishment, of trade union leaders through to the forcible suppression of strikes against very low wages and poor working conditions.

These MCF campaigns included mobilisations against particular examples of repression when colonial authorities were faced with movements for democracy and national liberation. For example, 11 prisoners of the independence movement in Kenya were beaten to death by prison guards in 1959 with many others suffering serious permanent injuries. The colonial authorities initially attempted a cover-up in response. But more information soon began to emerge. When this shameful episode was then debated in Parliament, support for the Kenya colony's administration was undermined, thereby accelerating moves towards Kenyan independence (finally achieved in 1963). Solidarity mobilisations in Britain were actively making a difference.

Sadly, this was far from being the only example of brutal repression carried out on behalf of the British government. Other instances included the example of Malaya, for instance, where trade unionists were being arrested and their federation banned in 1948. There followed detention without trial, and the 'resettling' of some 600,000 Malayans to 'new villages'. This was to prevent local people from providing supplies to the communist guerrillas/freedom fighters who were engaged in armed struggles against the colonial regime, only to have their bodies mutilated when they were killed by the British.

British interventions in Malaya were actually the subject of considera-tion at the T&G's biennial conference in Scarborough in 1949. Conference considered a motion calling for our troops to be brought out, with an end to what was being described as the 'British dictatorship', leading to the development of a democratic government based on universal suffrage. Although the motion was lost, this does point to the existence of support for colonial freedoms within the T&G at the time. The same biennial conference also passed motions in support of democracy in Spain and Greece – unanimously.

The history of British intervention in what was then British Guiana (now Guyana) in 1953 provides further evidence of the continuation of anti-democratic and colonial attitudes similarly influenced by Cold War concerns. The British government was not prepared to accept that British Guiana could enact a series of modest reforms, including legislation to ensure the right to trade union recognition, following the election of the People's Progressive Party under the leadership of Cheddi Jagan that year. Cheddi Jagan was alleged to be in receipt of 'red gold' from Moscow, a charge that he himself described as 'pure fantasy'.[10] No evidence was

10 Cheddi Jagan, *The West on Trial* (Michael Joseph, 1966), p.133.

produced and nor has any evidence been produced subsequently, just as in the case of the allegations against Albert Fava in Gibraltar.

British troops were sent in, all the same, on the very day that a Labour Relations Bill was being put together to force employers to negotiate with trade unions that had majority support amongst their workforces. Yet this intervention seems to have been accepted by the British TUC and the Labour Party, with a statement that 'instead of pursuing a policy of social reform and seeking to justify the faith placed in them by the electorate, the leaders of the People's Progressive Party (PPP) pursued a communist policy and created a situation which necessitated the movement of troops to ensure the maintenance of law and order'.[11] The TUC was specifically critical of the PPP's continuing contacts 'behind the Iron Curtain, with the WFTU rather than the International Federation of Free Trade Unions [ICFTU]'. There were, of course, objections from the Labour Left though.

The experiences of trade unionists in Gibraltar have already been cited to illustrate other, if less dramatically forceful examples of British resistance to movements for self-government – in this case with the active support of key figures within the T&G. But it is important to remember the history of the Left's opposition to British brutality in its colonies as well, along with their support for more progressive approaches to international solidarity and peace in Europe and elsewhere.

Fenner Brockway MP, the chair of the MCF exemplifies these links between support for movements for self-determination and movements for peace in the context of the Cold War. In addition to his support for the MCF, he was actively involved in campaigning for peace and for nuclear disarmament. And he went on to campaign against racism, including campaigning for legislation against racial discrimination (links with campaigns for racial equality that are to be explored more fully in the subsequent chapter). In summary, there was a significant basis for the development of alternative approaches to questions of colonial freedom, international solidarity and peace, along with questions of nuclear disarmament more specifically. Frank Cousins played a key role, building upon these foundations in the second part of the fifties. Much later, in 1969, he went on to become the first chair of the newly created Community Relations Council, further demonstrating his commitment to challenging racial discrimination along with his support for the movements for colonial liberation, peace and international solidarity.

11 Cheddi Jagan, *Forbidden Freedom* (Hansib, 1954), p.72.

The T&G and the Movement for Nuclear Disarmament

By the latter part of the fifties it was the question of nuclear disarmament that constituted the central focus in the context of these debates. Much of the scientific work that underpinned the development of the A (atomic) bomb had actually been carried out in Britain, but this research had been shared with the US which then put the research into practice with the bombing of Hiroshima and Nagasaki in the latter days of the Second World War. Since then there had been further developments in nuclear technology leading to the production of the massively more destructive H (hydrogen) bomb.

Ironically perhaps, given the extent of the British government's commitment to the US alliance and NATO, it was the Suez crisis in 1956 that has been identified as an additional factor in persuading Macmillan that Britain needed to continue to develop its own hydrogen bomb. Given the fiasco in Suez, perhaps the US was not such a reliable ally after all? Might it not be safer to press on with our own home-grown weapons of mass destruction? As it has already been suggested, Macmillan also seems to have thought that, however expensive this was going to be, the cost might still be less – and the weaponry more effective – than keeping so many troops on the ground across the globe, safeguarding Britain's (shrinking) colonial interests. The first British hydrogen bomb test was duly exploded in 1957. This galvanised the opposition into action. By the beginning of 1958 CND had been launched to campaign against the manufacture, deployment or use of nuclear weapons. Britain was being urged to take a moral lead here.

Frank Cousins was similarly clear that Britain should be taking such a moral lead – with the T&G taking a leading role, actively supporting the CND's objectives. Although he was personally sympathetic to a unilateralist position, he was also well aware that this view was far from universally supported within the T&G. Respecting this reality, he was therefore prepared to be somewhat circumspect in the ways in which he expressed the case for nuclear disarmament. As he himself pointed out, the T&G was 'not a Cousins' union. It is a members' union'.[12] His role in respecting and strengthening democracy within the T&G is explored more fully in Chapter 6.

Whilst respecting members' varying views, Frank Cousins did use his influence to make the case for nuclear disarmament to good effect though. He succeeded in persuading the 1959 biennial conference of this at Douglas, Isle of Man, describing nuclear weapons as 'not defence weapons' but 'weapons of mass suicide'.[13] As he had previously argued,

12 Stewart, *Frank Cousins*, p.21.
13 Murray, *The T&G Story*, p.123.

he saw no room for 'compromise with evil', emphasising 'the moral and political facets associated with the question of nuclear weapons'. Frank Cousins also reassured delegates, pointing to the motion's consistency with approaches that had already been agreed. And he carried the day – literally 'the day', the debate having lasted at length with the vote being adjourned until the following day.Nye Bevan was more doubtful however. He seems to have been concerned to maintain party unity as well as being anxious that such a position would prove to be a vote loser in the forthcoming general election. This was a view that was shared by Hugh Gaitskell, the Labour leader (who was personally opposed to the position in any case). In the event, the Labour Party did lose the 1959 general election. This paved the way for blame games to be played out, with Frank Cousins being identified as vote loser in chief, labelled as being responsible for alienating middle-class voters as a result of his position on nuclear disarmament, not to mention his support for the bus men's strike (already discussed in Chapter 2). Frank Cousins's biographer, Geoffrey Goodman, argues that there was not a scrap of evidence to support the view that nuclear disarmament was a vote loser in practice. But that didn't prevent the Right from interpreting events in this way. There would seem to be plenty of more recent parallels, as the discussion questions at the end of this chapter raise, for further reflection.

Meanwhile Frank Cousins pressed on with making the case for nuclear disarmament at the TUC, which passed two different motions, one from the T&G and one that reflected some remaining ambiguities it would seem. The issue was most certainly controversial on the Left more generally, with the Labour Party leader Hugh Gaitskell leading the charge from those who were vehemently opposed. By 1960, however, the case for nuclear disarmament was put by Frank Cousins, and carried at the Labour Party conference, despite Hugh Gaitskell's arguments to the contrary. This became a continuing bone of contention, along with the Labour Party's Clause 4 commitment to nationalisation, policies that Hugh Gaitskell pledged to continue to fight, 'and to fight and fight again to save the party we love' from the 'pacifists, unilateralists and fellow travellers' who were preaching disarmament and neutralism in the Cold War.[14] The connexions are all there then – anti-communism, the Cold War, disarmament and international peace. This battle for the soul of the Labour Party marks the end of this period of the T&G's history between 1945 and 1960, as the final chapter, Chapter 6, reflects in further detail.

14 Hennessy, *Having It So Good*, p.527.

Hugh Gaitskell
(1906–1963)

Hugh Gaitskell worked as a lecturer in political economy and as a wartime civil servant before going into Parliament as a Labour MP in 1945. This was under Clement Attlee's first government. He was rapidly promoted to become Minister of Fuel and Power, going on to become Chancellor of the Exchequer. When pressures for increased military spending grew in 1951, Hugh Gaitskell decided to find the money by cutting back on welfare spending, imposing the charges on dentures and glasses that led to Nye Bevan's resignation.

Hugh Gaitskell and Nye Bevan were long-standing rivals then, competing for the future direction of the Labour Party and the trade union and labour movement more generally. Hugh Gaitskell became leader of the Labour Party in 1955, leading the Party to defeat, yet again, in 1959. He and his supporters argued that the reason for this defeat was that the Labour Party was too far to the Left of the political spectrum. The Labour Party would only come to power again if there was a move to the centre ground. This was strongly contested from the Left.

As a result, there were major battles to follow. Hugh Gaitskell opposed the move towards support for unilateral nuclear disarmament, for example, a policy commitment that he succeeded in reversing eventually. He was less successful however, when it came to his attempts to remove Clause 4 of the Labour Party's constitution, providing for its principled commitment to nationalisation. The Left fought Gaitskell on this in what became described as a battle for the soul of the Labour Party.

Hugh Gaitskell was determined to fight on, to fight, fight, and fight again, as he put this himself. But without success. Clause 4 survived until the New Labour period. Hugh Gaitskell himself died in 1963. The Labour Party went on to win the following election with a programme of significant social reforms. Volume 4 continues the story of these struggles into the sixties.

Conclusions

Throughout this period between 1945 and 1960 the T&G played an extremely powerful leading role in the trade union and labour movement – for diametrically different policy aims and objectives. This was a story of two halves. The Churchillian Cold War policies that were pursued by Ernest Bevin and Arthur Deakin dominated the first half only to be dramatically reversed with the election of Frank Cousins as general secretary in 1956. From then on into the sixties, the T&G led the way, promoting policies for peace and international solidarity. As a result the international impact of the T&G can scarcely be exaggerated,.

As Frank Cousins himself has been quoted as pointing out though, this dramatic turnaround needs to be understood in its wider context both within the union and outside it more generally. Dissatisfaction with the politics of the Deakin era had already been growing, dissatisfaction that applied to international policies as well as to domestic policy approaches. And just as the Left, particularly the Left rank and file, had become increasingly critical in the Deakin years, so the Right continued to mobilise when Frank Cousins became general secretary. Many of the full-time officials who had been appointed in the Deakin years continued in their posts as well, continuing to exercise considerable influence from the Right.

These continuing debates between Left and Right approaches were mirrored more widely, as the battles for the soul of the Labour Party so clearly demonstrated at the end of this period. Volume 4 follows these battles further, into the sixties and beyond.

Meanwhile the following chapter traces similar although far from identical debates in relation to equalities issues within the T&G, in the context of the migrations that followed from Britain's imperial legacies in the fifties, whether these were legacies of violence and oppression, or legacies of underdevelopment, unemployment and poverty – or both. The links between Britain's imperial past and the migrations that followed have been summarised succinctly by anti-racist activists as follows: 'We are here because you were there'.

But first, before moving on to the impact in terms of struggles for equalities in Britain, some questions for further consideration.

Questions for Discussion: Chapter 3

- How far would you agree with the view that trade unions should refrain from raising controversial issues that might be vote losers in the run up to a general election?

- Do you agree or disagree with the view that the threats that were posed in the Cold War period were actually much exaggerated?

- How would you evaluate the view that Britain (still) needs nuclear weapons in order to have 'a seat of the top table'?

- Do you have any further thoughts about the quotation from Palme Dutt that was posed at the end of the previous chapter?

4

Struggles for Equalities

As Frank Cousins's career as a trade union leader has already demonstrated in the previous chapter, struggles for equalities in Britain have been inextricably linked with the trade union and labour movement's struggles for international solidarity and peace. There was a logic to Cousins becoming chair of the Community Relations Council after so many years supporting struggles for human rights across the globe. This chapter moves on to focus on the T&G's involvement istruggles for equalities back here at home in Britain.

The chapter begins by outlining the context for race relations in Britain in the post-war period, setting the framework for debates within the trade union and labour movement in general and the T&G more specifically. How did these debates translate into trade union policies as expressed via the decisions of biennial conferences? And what were the effects in relation to struggles for equalities within particular industries and localities?

The 1948 Nationality Act provides a starting point for these debates (with Attlee revealed as seemingly complicit in implicitly racist agendas, although anxious not to appear to be so). These issues are set out in the context of debates about decolonisation together with debates about the arrival of Commonwealth citizens in search of employment from the late forties onwards. Case studies include struggles against the Far Right and anti-Semitism in the immediate post-war period, along with struggles against racism, including struggles against effective colour bars, into the fifties and beyond.

The chapter then moves on to explore struggles for women's equality in the workplace. Unequal pay and struggles to achieve equalities were successively debated and re-affirmed at biennial conferences – with continuing problems when it came to turning these aspirations into effect. And there were struggles for women to remain in the workforce at all, after the Second World War, challenges for women workers that were compounded by the closures of wartime nurseries and other support services.

Meanwhile there were various moves to support the growing numbers of women members within the T&G itself, including moves to engage women in trade union education, moves that are explored more fully in Chapter 5. Despite these initiatives, and despite so many examples of women playing leading roles in industrial struggles more generally, the T&G remained overwhelmingly male at the top, however. There was barely a woman in sight, let alone a woman of colour, judging from the photos of biennial conferences between 1947 and 1959. The struggle for equalities has been a continuing theme running throughout this period and beyond – unfinished business as subsequent volumes testify.

Legacies of the Second World War

The Second World War was profoundly important in terms of its impacts, as previous chapters have already illustrated. Struggles for colonial freedom had been given impetus. People of colour had come to Britain, serving in the armed forces, many coming back again subsequently, pressured by the dearth of employment opportunities back home, encouraged to fill the yawning gaps in the labour market here in Britain.

Meanwhile women had been drawn into the labour force during the war, taking up jobs that had previously been regarded as men's preserve. Many were understandably reluctant to return to more traditional roles in the home when this was proposed in the post-war period. Women's employment actually grew from the fifties, despite these pressures. Women had gained confidence as well as gaining knowledge and skills through their wartime experiences.

So had many men. The results could be seen in the post-war period more generally. There was widespread understanding of the arguments for social reforms along the lines of the Beveridge Report, outlining the thinking behind the establishment of the post-war welfare state. And there was evidence of greater confidence amongst rank-and-file trade unionists, more specifically, helping to explain the growth of the shop stewards' movement during this period. The extent of such influences may be a matter of debate. But the following example of anti-fascist mobilisations by Jewish ex-service men and ex-service women would certainly seem to provide evidence in support of such views.

Mobilisations Against the Far Right
in the Immediate Post-War Period

Fascism was supposed to have been defeated but the post-war reality was something else again. When they returned to civilian life just after the close of the Second World War, a group of Jewish veterans discovered that, for all the efforts and sacrifice, Oswald Mosley and his gangs of fascists were still harassing Jewish communities in London and elsewhere.[1] They were getting away with proclaiming appalling anti-Semitic slogans on street corners such as that 'Not enough Jews were burnt at Belsen'. So, these Jewish veterans decided that their days of fighting fascism were far from being over. The 43 Group was formed to stop this resurgence of the Far Right, 'by any means necessary'. The veterans included women as well as men, described as being highly organised and well-trained. And they were confident and determined in their commitment to stop the fascists in their tracks.

The 43 Group was named after the number of those initially involved, according to one account (although this account of the group's origins has been challenged, suggesting that '43' was actually the number of the room in which they first met – illustrating some of the potential limitations of relying on individual memories via oral history more generally perhaps). However that may be, the 43 Group soon grew, with hundreds of members mobilising to take action, from heckling at fascist meetings to taking on more directly physical challenges when confronted with fascist violence; as happened at 'the Battle of Ridley Road Market' in East London in 1947 for example.

Whilst physical violence tended to be most evident in poorer working-class places such as London's East End, anti-Semitism was not simply confined to these areas. It is important to remember the extent to which anti-Semitism was supported amongst the British upper classes and indeed amongst the middle classes too. In 1945 there was an 'anti-alien' petition calling for Jewish refugees to be moved out of Hampstead to make room for ex-service personnel, for example – although this petition was also contested at the time. The extent to which there was support for anti-Semitism across social classes needed to be taken seriously and challenged during this period then – as indeed it still does.

The 43 Group itself included activists who subsequently became known for very different reasons, including the hairdresser Vidal Sassoon. They included active trade unionists, including a number of taxi drivers, many of whom would have been members of the T&G. They played key roles, providing information about fascist mobilisations, giving lifts and tip offs, transporting activists to the scenes of fascist mobilisations and, most importantly, being on hand to drive activists to safety when needed. Understandably there is little in the way of direct information about T&G members carrying out these functions, as Danny Freeman, currently education and development organiser for the London and Eastern Region of Unite, discovered when researching this topic. As his study of the

---

1 Morris Beckman, *The 43 Group* (History Press, 2013); Daniel Sonabend, *We Fight Against Fascists* (Verso, 2019).

43 Group and the London taxi trade so clearly pointed out, going public would have put a taxi driver's badge – and therefore his livelihood – on the line.[2] Some 60 years later, one of the former activists that Danny Freeman interviewed still preferred to remain anonymous – fearing attacks from more recently formed groupings of the Far Right. Much of the information that did exist had been destroyed in any case, when the group disbanded in 1950, after Mosely's departure with his tail between his legs.

By 1950, Mosely's fascists seemed to have been defeated. This was for a number of reasons. There were new targets for the Far Right to attack, with the arrival of Black migrants from the Caribbean, on the 'Empire Windrush'. And there were, of course, the courageous mobilisations of the 43 Group of Jewish ex-servicemen and women to take into account.[3] The extent of their impact may be hard to verify, relying, as subsequent accounts do, on somewhat limited information. But the 43 Group does seem to have acted as the spearhead of resistance to the Far Right, along with anti-fascist mobilisations from other sections of the Left more generally, including Hackney Trades Council and the Communist Party. The strength of their determination and commitment had been extraordinary, qualities that were to be needed time and again in subsequent mobilisations to tackle racism and anti-Semitism in their varying guises, as these have emerged and re-emerged across social classes in Britain over time.

The Policy Context on Immigration and Race

So where was the Labour government in all this? Attlee has been criticised for not taking a clear enough stand on anti-Semitism in the immediate post-war period. As the issue of immigration emerged on the public policy agenda soon after, Labour's response seems to have been similarly ambivalent, if not actually downright racist. George Padmore – a leading international activist – wrote to Attlee in 1945, making the case for colonial freedom as well as making the case for laws against racial discrimination back home in Britain. It seems that Attlee didn't reply. The previous chapter has already outlined the Labour government's resistance to colonial freedom unless this was seen as absolutely necessary (as in the case of the Indian sub-continent).

Official attitudes towards immigration and racial discrimination in Britain were profoundly contradictory. On the one hand there were labour shortages, including shortages of skilled labour, hence the 1948 British Nationality Act, encouraging migration from the Commonwealth. But

2 Danny Freeman, '*Never Again!*': *The 43 Group and the Role of the London Taxi Trade* (MA thesis, London Metropolitan University, 2014).

3 See Beckman's account of his own experiences in the 43 Group; Beckman, *The 43 Group*.

there was implicit, if not actually explicit, racism on the other hand. It seems that those who drafted the 1948 Act hadn't appreciated that white people 'of British stock' (as they were being described) were not the only ones with the skills that were being sought. Black people had skills too. Correspondence has subsequently been unearthed, pointing to some official embarrassment, wanting to contain Black immigration but not wanting to be seen to be overtly racist. Subsequently, in the early 1950s, Churchill actually asked government officials if they could identify a way to keep West Indians out of the country, despite the 1948 Nationality Act, targeting non-white immigrants whilst not appearing to be motivated by racial considerations.[4]

Meanwhile there was active recruitment in the Caribbean with Enoch Powell amongst those seeking to encourage migration, in this particular case encouraging nurses from Barbados to come to fill gaps in the NHS's labour force. To describe the policy context as ambivalent seems something of an understatement then. Eleven Labour MPs actually wrote to Attlee asking him to control Black immigration to Britain. George Isaacs, Minister of Labour in the Attlee government at the time (and general secretary of the print union, NATSOPA from 1909) apparently stressed that the West Indians who arrived on the Empire Windrush had *not* been officially invited, hoping that no encouragement would be given to others to follow their example. Britain wanted West Indians' labour evidently – but not their black skins amongst us.

But this was as nothing compared to some of the attitudes that were being expressed amongst the Conservatives in the post-war period, with Lord Salisbury warning of the potential horrors of a 'magpie' nation, and Churchill apparently toying with the idea of fighting the 1955 general election on the slogan of 'Keep England White' (the concern with 'England' per se; so how much of this particular brand of xenophobic nationalism was about 'Little England' rather than the rest of Britain?). The connections with Britain's colonial past are only too evident, in any case here, ruling over colonies that did have colour bars in practice, particularly where there were white settlers who were determined to protect their positions from Black competition, as in Kenya and Southern Rhodesia (now Zimbabwe) for example. Perhaps unsurprisingly given such attitudes – and such political leadership from the top, there were instances of racist violence in response to the arrival of these newcomers, with hostels accommodating Black sailors being attacked in Liverpool, for example. But despite this, immigration continued, with immigration from the Caribbean rising from 2,000 in 1953 to 27,000 in 1955 – with further racist violence to come with the Notting Hill race riots of 1958, just as one specific example.

The Caribbean arrivals were of course only one element in the pattern of immigration from Commonwealth countries in the post-war period.

4 David Olusoga, *Black and British* (Macmillan, 2016).

Migrants arrived from South Asia in particular, including migrants from Pakistan, as well as migrants who had suffered displacement, fleeing the massacres that followed the botched partition of India at the time of Indian independence. There were strong links between these immigration patterns and Britain's colonial past, as it has already been suggested, along with continuing links with racism – and anti-racism – within the trade union and labour movement and wider society. Volume 4 explores the impact of migration from South Asia and elsewhere, including its impact on the labour force in the foundries and the car components industries in the Midlands, for example, in the following decade.

Trade Union Policies on Racism in the Post-War Period

Reports from the T&G's biennial conferences illustrate these competing ideas about race, colonialism and migration as they were played out in public debates. For example, an early conference motion on foreign labour argued that 'until the policy of full employment has been fulfilled we reject the Labour government's proposals for foreign labour to be imported into industry'.[5] Clearly there were concerns about the possible threats that migration from the Commonwealth may have been posing to jobs, pay and conditions, concerns with potentially racist undertones. But the motion in question was lost, anyway.

At the following conference, in Scarborough in 1949, a resolution in support of getting troops out of Malaya – replacing the British 'dictator-ship' with a democratic government elected on the basis of universal suffrage – was also lost. But motions supporting democracy in Spain and Greece were passed unanimously, as the previous chapter has already pointed out. Democracy in Europe was fine apparently, just not so essential in Britain's colonies perhaps? As for freedom from colonial rule, this was evidently still too contentious as well.

At the biennial conference in Southsea in 1953 there were expressions of similarly competing perspectives within the T&G. There was a motion condemning the colour bar. Conference reaffirmed 'its belief in the universal brotherhood [sic] of man and its endorsement of the Human Rights Charter of the United Nations Organisation'. Discrimination on the grounds of race or colour was described as being 'unchristian and contrary to trade union principles'. However, Conference also recognised 'the grave situation which is revealed by uncontrolled immigration from any source'. Especially when migrants leave home because of unemployment (a key driver in the Caribbean), they often arrive 'ignorant of and unprepared for the great differences in climate and in social custom which greet them'. They were

---

5 MRC MSS.126/TG/1887/12. Minutes and Record of the 12th Biennial Delegate Conference, 1947.

often exploited, the motion argued (which indeed they were). So Conference was urged to call on government to work out a policy with the TUC based on 'the control of immigration in such a manner as will overcome these evils', along with investment in the West Indies and other colonial territories 'thereby eliminating the need to emigrate merely for the purpose of securing the right to live'.[6] This was carried unanimously. The biennial conference in Blackpool in 1955 expressed similar concerns about imported labour – whilst reaffirming the T&G's opposition to the colour bar.

In summary then, the T&G was clearly opposed to racism. Or was it? There was some evidence of support for movements for colonial freedom and democracy along with opposition to the colour bar, more specifically, both in Britain and elsewhere. But there was also evidence of concerns about the possible effects of migration, on jobs, pay and conditions. Such concerns could easily morph into racist attitudes and behaviours. And employers could easily play upon such fears, just as they could – and did – play upon fears about women workers as potential threats to men, as the subsequent section of this chapter illustrates, 'playing divide and rule' tactics at home here in Britain, just as the colonisers had been doing, dividing populations across the British Empire in previous years.

Racism and Anti-Racist Struggles in Practice

Unsurprisingly – given the wider political and policy backgrounds – these differences can be identified through the histories of specific disputes. Migration and race were highly contentious, and potentially very divisive issues. As a Communist Party pamphlet from 1955 argued: 'The arrival of some thousands of West Indians has, as most people know, been made the occasion of attempts to set white people against black, to impose a colour bar, to persuade all kinds of people that their homes or their jobs are endangered'.[7] But this was simply not true, in the writer's view. As the pamphlet went on to point out 'It was not the presence of coloured workers that put 2 million people out of jobs during the nineteen thirties', going on to argue for solidarity with the colonial people who were coming to Britain. They came for better livelihoods, Britain having ignored their needs back home in the colonies themselves. 'Employers may try to use coloured labour to undercut wages' the pamphlet continued, so the answer was to recruit them into trade unions, on the basis of 'United We Stand, Divided We Fall'.

There were indeed examples of trade union resistance to racism, including examples of resistance to attempts to divide workers along

6 MRC MSS.126/TG/1887/15. Record of the 15th Biennial Delegate Conference, 1953.

7 Philip Bolsover, *No Colour Bar for Britain* (Communist Party of Great Britain, 1955), p.3.

racist lines within the T&G – just as there were examples of the opposite. London Transport was a case in point. There were labour shortages on the buses in the post-war period, the result of the relative unattractiveness of the wages on offer, along with the shift patterns that were inherent in the jobs. London Transport's attempts to recruit women as bus conductors were resisted at first because of fears that women were being used as part of management's strategies to depress wages and conditions (as the subsequent section of this chapter explores in further detail). There were parallel fears when London Transport decided to recruit from the Caribbean, setting up a recruitment office in Barbados. This was seen as a potential threat to trade union organisation more generally too.

The reality was very different, in practice, however, as the level of solidarity in the 1958 bus strike that was discussed in Chapter 2 demonstrated. Black and white workers stood together throughout. But this did not prevent the London Bus Conference subsequently passing a resolution opposing the influx of immigrants to this country and their employment in London Transport'.

There were significant differences both within and between workplaces on these issues. In Birmingham, Liverpool and Nottingham Black workers were employed as bus conductors and some were employed as drivers. The T&G in Liverpool specifically welcomed them. But experiences in Bristol were more mixed.

The Bristol bus boycott was organised in protest against Bristol Omnibus's long-standing ban on employing Black bus crews. The leaders of this boycott drew upon experiences from elsewhere, as they developed this tactic, specifically drawing on the lessons of struggles for civil rights in the US at this time. The Bristol boycott lasted for four months before being successfully concluded with support from white activists as well as from Black activists. The boycott itself took place in 1963, making this a subject for the following volume. But the origins go back to the 1950s.

Madge Dresser's account of the background to this particular struggle starts from white Bristolians anxieties about jobs. But she also notes the resentments that some white people felt when they saw Black men dancing with white girls. This seemed to spark off very particular anxieties and jealousies. Whatever the reasons, however rational or emotional, there were divisions on the issue of Black crews within the T&G. In 1955 there was a ballot of busmen in the Passenger Group of the T&G in Bristol, with a majority coming out against the employment of Black bus crews. But the maintenance section voted the other way.

Meanwhile management effectively stirred the situation further by announcing that they were fine with hiring Black staff. It was the T&G that was not. This management claim was denied, however, the regional officer arguing that the T&G was not actually opposed to the recruitment of Black busmen. On the contrary, he pointed out, there was no colour bar in place, going on to point out that '[w]e have a lot of coloured members in Bristol, most of them on the labouring side' (including several hundred Black T&G members at Fry's chocolate factory in the area).[8] But the regional secretary was still criticised for not taking a clearer stand or challenging the Passenger Division's motion on the colour bar on the buses. The fact is that this particular regional secretary had only taken up office in 1957, two years after the said motion. But he had attempted to downplay the issue in order to defend the union's reputation, it was argued by his critics, rather than challenging racism head on.

The local branch of the T&G refused to meet with a delegation from the West Indian Development Council, and an increasingly bitter war of words was fought out in the local media. Ron Nethercott, South West regional secretary of the union, persuaded a local Black T&G member, Bill Smith, to sign a statement which called for quiet negotiations to solve the dispute. It condemned Paul Stephenson of the West Indian Development Council for causing potential harm to the city's Black and Asian popula-tion. Nethercott went on to launch an attack on Stephenson in the *Daily Herald* newspaper, calling him dishonest and irresponsible. This led to a libel case in the High Court, which awarded Stephenson damages and costs in December 1963. Bristol Trades Council condemned the T&G on this as a result. This was a seriously unhappy episode for the union. Many years later, in February 2013, Unite issued an apology for their predecessor T&G's unacceptable handling of the bus boycott.

In the event, the campaign against the colour bar on Bristol's buses attracted high-profile support, including support from the Black activist Claudia Jones and the West Indian cricket hero, Leary Constantine, as well as attracting support from Tony Benn (then a local MP), Fenner Brockway and Harold Wilson. This was in addition to widespread support from both Black and white trade unionists and community activists. The details of the campaign's success belong, however, to the subsequent volume.

Meanwhile, in the introduction to her account, Madge Dresser points to the importance of the lessons to be learned. It was, she emphasised, her fervent hope that this was not dismissed as union bashing. 'True it does expose the racism and insensitivity which existed amongst the rank and file bus crews' she continued. 'But it also shows how much such attitudes were grounded in fears about economic security at a time of great social and cultural change'. She went on to acknowledge the spirit of solidarity amongst bus crews subsequently (she was writing in the eighties), pointing to the ways in which the regional and national leaderships of the T&G were evolving their own policies against racism. Her hope was that her account would be of use to them as part of these processes,[9] processes with relevance for equalities struggles more generally in the years to follow.

---

8 Madge Dresser, *Black and White on the Buses* (Bristol Broadsides, 1986), p.14.

9 Dresser, *Black and White on the Buses*, p.5.

The Policy Context for Women's Equality

There are parallels as well as differences when it comes to understanding the policy context for women's struggles for equality within the workplace. There were comparable levels of ambivalence for a start. There was some recognition of the arguments in favour of equal pay for equal work. And there was evidence of official resistance, just as there was resistance to the idea that married women should continue to work outside the home, especially if they had young children.

Attitudes within the trade union movement were also ambivalent, with fears that employers would try to use women's employment to undercut wages and conditions for men. But women's labour was definitely in demand, in order to cope with the labour shortages that followed the Second World War. Women's participation in the labour force actually increased over this period, particularly part-time work, which had been consciously preferred as the solution to the problem of women's double burden, enabling them to combine their family responsibilities with their roles in the labour force. And as women's participation in the labour force grew, so did women's membership in the T&G.

As previous volumes have already outlined, the demand for equal pay for equal work has a long history in the trade union and labour movement (although this was not yet being defined as 'work of equal value', a crucial distinction that was added to make equal pay legislation more effective, in later years, as subsequent volumes explain in further detail). Unsurprisingly, given the amazing contributions that women had made to the economy during the war, the issue of equal pay for equal work emerged again in the post-war period. Women would expect some practical recognition of their work for the war effort, whether directly in the armed forces and/or in arms production, including aircraft production, for example, or less directly through the Land Army, keeping food production going and by supporting the war effort in other ways through the Women's Voluntary Service for Civil Defence (WVS) which had over a million members by 1942. Women had been gaining in confidence and their collective sense of worth as a result of these experiences during the war, it has been argued (Jones, 2000).[10]

Reflecting on these experiences, women commented on their feelings about working in these new situations. 'We were happy working' as a woman who had been a firewatcher and factory worker explained. 'I don't think we went back to the fireside in the same way again'.[11] 'The war was good for being able to get money', a woman who had been working in engineering

---

10 Helen Jones, *Women in British Public Life* (Longman, 2000).
11 Pam Schweitzer, Lorraine Hilton and Jane Moss, *What Did You Do in the War, Mum?* (Age Exchange Theatre Company, 1985), p.41.

commented in similar vein. 'We'd got our independence during the war', she added, 'and what we didn't have then, we made sure we got after'.[12]

So how did the Attlee government respond to these raised aspirations for the right to work and for the right to be paid equally for equal work? Supportively – or not so supportively? As the Chancellor of the Exchequer announced in 1947: 'The Government accepts as regards their own employees the justice of the claim' (for equal pay for work of equal value) which was a step forward for civil servants. But the government was not prepared to apply the principle more widely, this announcement continued, on the grounds that this would be inflationary. Once again, as Chapter 2 has already outlined, it was to be the workers who should bear the costs of Britain's economic problems in the post-war period, only it was to be women workers in the private sector who should shoulder the burden in this particular instance.

The Attlee government was actually ambivalent about the role of married women in the labour force at all. However much their contributions had been welcomed in wartime, this was all set to change. Already, back in 1945, the Ministry of Health had sent around a circular that contained the following section.

The Ministers concerned accept the view of medical and other authority that, in the interests of the health and development of the child no less than for the benefit of the mother, the proper place for a child under two is at home with his [sic] mother'. 'They are also of the opinion that under peacetime conditions the right policy to pursue would be positively to discourage mothers of children under two from going out to work.[13]

The General Council of the TUC actually agreed with this position in principle, as the 1948 annual report explained: home was one of the most important spheres for women and it would be doing a great injury to the life of the nation if women were persuaded or forced to neglect their domestic duties in order to enter industry particularly when there were young children to cater for. This underlying philosophy was largely unchallenged until the late 1960s, however unrealistic, or indeed unwelcome this was for so many women.

The Beveridge Report that had outlined the principles of the welfare state for the post-war period had actually gone even further. It was not only women with young children who should stay at home. The entire social insurance system was based on the principle of the male breadwinner

---

12 Schweitzer et al., *What Did You Do*, p.52.
13 Ministry of Health and Ministry of Education, Nursery Provision for Children Under Five. Circular 221/45 (London: HMSO, 1945).

bringing home the family wage. He would bring home the bacon or be the one to qualify for social insurance benefits, if need be. The assumption was that married women would be economically dependent on their husbands. Once the war was won, it was assumed, the situation would revert to 'normal' i.e. the men would return from the forces and their wives would stay home to care for their families. So, the nurseries and nursery classes that had been set up in wartime could be closed along with the canteens that had enabled food to be prepared most effectively, freeing up working women from the challenges of cooking in times of rationing. It would be down to local authorities to organise such nursery facilities as they still deemed necessary for their areas.

Everything was to be as it was. Except that it wasn't always like this idealised vision of the family in the past. Working-class women had so often worked in the past anyway, even if their work had been less visible – work such as taking in laundry, for example. As one of the women who contributed to a collection of stories about what they had done during the war commented: 'For women it was marvellous that they could get away from home, but it was more so for the upper middle class families where the daughter was stuck at home until she married'. They (i.e. upper middle-class women) had no idea that working-class women had actually always worked, however. 'We had to, we couldn't have kept our families without'.[14]

No wonder that women criticised the Beveridge Report at the time, just as women subsequently continued to campaign for the services that had made it so much easier for them to work. But before coming on to women's responses and the role of the T&G, it is important to summarise the ambiguity that was still inherent in government approaches to the question of women working, just as there had been ambiguity when it had come to the demand for migrant labour. Married women should be at home – except when their labour was needed for the good of the national economy. Maybe there would be cases when extra funding would be needed to meet extra needs, it was conceded.

The government evidently wanted to have it both ways, mothers as domestic goddesses in the home AND women at work, filling vital gaps in the labour force in the pursuit of national economic recovery – ideology versus practical economics?

There had certainly been a strong ideological dimension to the Beveridge Report itself, just as there was a strong ideological component to the closure of nursery facilities and the drive – even if this was a somewhat ambivalent drive – to get married women back into the home. As Fiona Williams's study of social policy has commented, despite the importance of the reforms that the Beveridge Report presented, 'national

---

14 Schweitzer et al., *What Did You Do*, p.42–43.

and male chauvinism were built into the structure of these provisions'.[15] Beveridge himself was on record as arguing that: '[t]he attitude of the housewife to gainful employment outside the home is not and should not be the same as that of the single woman. She (i.e. the married woman) has other duties', Beveridge argued, going on to explain that 'Mothers have vital work to do in ensuring the adequate continuance of the British Race and of British Ideals in the world'.[16] (As others have already commented, it is all there, nationalism, imperialism and male chauvinism, intertwined in a ghastly cocktail of prejudices.)

T&G Responses to Women's Demands

The T&G already had a history of recruiting women, with increasing recognition of the importance of their membership, as evidenced by the establishment of the first women's conference in 1943. And there had been recognition of the need for more nursery provision, including nursery provision for part-time women workers during the war. The T&G had actually taken the lead in pressing engineering employers for an agreement for part-time workers, for instance, setting the ball rolling as one historian described this. Overall then, the T&G's record has been described as having much to be proud of.[17] And the T&G did have much to be proud of – even if this was only part of the story, as subsequent examples illustrate. The reality was more complex.

Despite previous commitments during the war, the enthusiasm of the leadership towards organising women workers has been described as beginning to cool, as the country began to return to the 'normality' of men in work and women in the home. By March 1946, there were 159,090 women in membership compared with 215,199 at the end of 1944, a reduction of 56,049, at a time when the union's membership was growing overall.

Nevertheless, there was still pressure to build on the scope for growth in the new industries like electronics, as well as to maintain the involvement of women in the mainstream of the union. In the new industrial areas, building women's organisation in the engineering trade group was an important priority. For a start, there were companies like Ever Ready at Dagenham and Tottenham and Halex in Chingford with large numbers of women workers to be organised.

Women's membership in fact grew steadily throughout the 1950s, although women were still a relatively small proportion of the total

15 Fiona Williams, *Social Policy* (Polity, 1989), p.161–162
16 Elizabeth Wilson, *Women and the Welfare State* (Tavistock, 1977), pp.151–152.
17 Murray, *The T&G Story.*

membership of 1,328,820 in 1956, only 8,240 short of the figure for 1951. By early 1957 women's membership had grown again to 163,361, a total increase of 8,101 over the previous two years.

So how was the T&G responding to women's demands in this shifting, contradictory post-war period? Whether there was some cooling off amongst the leadership or not, the T&G was still supporting women's demands for the services that were needed to enable them to work. At the 1945 Biennial Conference, Deakin explained that he had written to government ministers in support of a resolution that:

> regrets the policy now being pursued in relation to the closing down of day and residential nurseries, the nurseries having played such an important part during the war years in enabling mothers with young children to return to employment, satisfied that their children were being properly cared for.[18]

This conference resolution had continued as follows, urging the government 'to encourage local authorities in every possible way to reopen those nurseries which have been closed, and to extend the number wherever these are necessary, and to develop nursery school facilities in order to enable mothers to return to employment if they desire to do so'.[19]

The National Delegate Conference of Women Members that was organised in 1947 focused on equal pay for equal work. This event was attended by 121 delegates, plus Florence Hancock, along with other officials and the general secretary. In his speech to the conference, Deakin identified equal pay as a class issue, and not a gender issue, defining this as follows:

> The question arises as to what we mean when we use this term. I want to give you the answer to that question. It simply means that irrespective of sex, those who do precisely the same work should receive the same rate of pay [...] it refers to the rate for the job. There is no ambiguity about that.[20]

This was a demand that had already been partially accepted in some areas of employment during the war years, but not in others, leaving open the possibilities – and fears – of 'dilution' i.e. women workers (as well as men) being employed to take on the less skilled tasks of skilled work, supervised by skilled or semi-skilled workers. This was seen as

18 MRC MSS.126/TG/1887/11. Record of the 11th Biennial Delegate Conference, 1945.
19 MRC MSS.126/TG/1887/11. Record of the 11th Biennial Delegate Conference, 1945.
20 MRC MSS.126/TG/RES/X/749B1. Record of National Delegate Conference of Women Members, 1947.

potentially undermining skilled rates of pay and therefore unacceptable. No wonder that Deakin made positive references to the union's work 'on behalf of women in industry, and [...] to the efforts consistently made to establish the principle of equal pay for equal work'[21] when he addressed the 1947 National Delegate Conference of Women Members.

Deakin was also aware of another factor that in his view needed to be taken into account. There were labour shortages that were identified as impeding Britain's economic recovery. His address to the conference was reported as going on to deal with 'the position confronting the country at this time, with particular reference to the inadequacy of the labour force and pointed to the urgent need for attracting women back into industry'.[22] The conference duly passed a resolution in support of equal pay, along with the importance of supporting women's contributions to the economy at this time, as follows.

That this National Delegate Conference of Women Members of the Transport and General Workers Union expresses the view that every effort should be made to secure the greatest possible use of our woman power as a contribution to helping the country in its grave economic situation. We urge that in all relevant negotiations the practicality of utilising woman power should be stressed, their employment to be on terms of equality of opportunity and 'The Rate for the Job'.

'We believe that to operate to the full a Socialist programme' this resolution continued, 'every available pair of hands will be needed, so that our standard of living can be sustained and improved'. [23]

The resolution went on to urge the government to implement equal pay across the public sector as an example to other employers, as well as urging the GEC to seek 'to eradicate the anomaly which continues to class women as the "poor relations' of industry"'.[24]

Strong views were expressed during the debate that followed. Deakin agreed with the women's demands though, adding that success depended on building strong organisation amongst women. Needs must?[25]

21 MRC MSS.126/TG/RES/X/749B1. Record of National Delegate Conference of Women Members, 1947.
22 MRC MSS.126/TG/RES/X/749B1. Record of National Delegate Conference of Women Members, 1947.
23 MRC MSS.126/TG/RES/X/749B1. Record of National Delegate Conference of Women Members, 1947.
24 MRC MSS.126/TG/RES/X/749B1. Record of National Delegate Conference of Women Members, 1947.
25 MRC MSS.126/TG/RES/X/749B1. Record of National Delegate Conference of Women Members, 1947.

Meanwhile this women's conference demonstrated its wider interests too, taking up a range of issues of particular concern to women members. As with previous discussions in 1945, the 1947 conference went on to pass resolutions on day nurseries and nursery schools. And the conference addressed issues of health and welfare, including the need for civic restaurants to meet the requirements of modern industry, along with the need for effective price controls on housing, on foodstuffs such as green vegetables and on household goods, as well as making the case for controls on profits.

There were, in addition, calls for weekend schools for women, and for more women officers in the union. Perhaps unsurprisingly this latter demand was more problematic for the leadership. Not a lot happened in terms of the appointment of more women officers. The view of Deakin and the GEC has been described as the classic defence against positive discrimination. When the issue was raised subsequently it was felt that although the GEC understood that specialist women officers would be an advantage, they felt that women members were in a no less favourable position than male members in that all vacancies were open to all members of the appropriate trade sections irrespective of sex. So, there wasn't a problem? Or was there? The GEC that was elected in 1950 reverted to being all male.

Although T&G officials, and indeed most shop stewards, were predominantly male at this time – not all of them supportive of women's demands by any manner of means – there were some (if not so many) prominent women officials. Amongst these was Florence Hancock, the national woman's officer, along with Ellen McCullough, whose contributions to T&G's educational programmes emerge in more detail in the following chapter. In summary then, despite being in a minority, in terms of T&G's leading positions women were clearly putting their demands forward with vigour, keen to play fuller roles as active trade unionists for the future, with more opportunities for trade union education, and with more women in key positions within the union.

Women's Issues As These Were Discussed
at T&G Biennial Conferences

Women were actively involved in raising their issues at T&G biennial conferences, more generally as well as within the National Delegate Conference of Women Members, flagging up the importance of women members' concerns, and indeed of women's membership and participation in the T&G per se. It was Florence Hancock who raised the issue of women's membership, and the importance of increasing this, at the biennial conference in Hastings in 1947. Despite the increases of the peak war years, '[w]e cannot regard our membership amongst women as satisfactory' she pointed out. 'Notwithstanding the drift of women from

Dame Florence May Hancock (1893–1974)

Figure 7: Florence Hancock, National Women's Officer

Hancock was born in Chippenham in 1893 to a family of cloth weavers. Her interest in trade unions and workers' rights was apparently sparked off by her father, who took her to hear David Lloyd George when she was around the age of 10.

She started work in Chippenham's Waverley cafe, at the age of 12 before taking a job for Nestlé in a factory making condensed milk. In 1913, she was a founding member of a branch of the Workers' Union there. When the sacking of two other founder members led to a strike, she played a prominent role.

Florence Hancock went on to join the Independent Labour Party in 1915. She became a full-time district organiser for the Workers' Union, which joined with the T&G. in 1929. She subsequently served as the National Women's Officer of the T&G from 1942, actively campaigning for women's rights at work.

She also became involved in the campaign for the TUC to create a women's section. When it did so she served on the committee, and then from 1935 on the General Council of the TUC. The TUC appointed her as their delegate to the International Labour Organization. In 1947/8, she served as president of the TCU.

As the 1950s drew to a close, so did the career of Florence Hancock, still the national women's officer. She was by now even more part of the establishment, involving herself in events such as the first Duke of Edinburgh's 'Study conference on human problems in industry' in 1956 where she represented the TUC on the conference organising council. In that year she was also invited to join the Board of the BBC. Her retirement took effect from 1958.

industry following the end of the war', she continued, 'there is still a vast field for recruitment' with labour shortages likely to lead to 'a substantial return of women to industry'.[26]

Married women had been leaving work and some women had been going back to their former jobs, with different trade union memberships, the Women's Section recognised. But in their view women should be encouraged to return to work and given training opportunities. And for this to happen there needed to be good canteens and more nursery schools, day nurseries and play centres.

Unsurprisingly the issue of pay was also central to the concerns that were raised at biennial conferences. There had been expressions of great disappointment that the Royal Commission on Equal Pay had been so unhelpful in its conclusions (the majority report having failed to agree to support the case for implementing equal pay for equal work in the then current economic circumstances). A motion supporting equal pay for equal work was passed unanimously at this biennial conference.

This support was repeated at subsequent biennial conferences. In 1953 there was again unanimous support for a motion supporting 'equal pay for women when engaged on work similar to that performed by men', with calls for strong representations on this issue. Similar motions were passed at the 1955 biennial conference in Blackpool, the 1957 biennial conference in Torquay and the Douglas, Isle of Man biennial conference in 1959.

So how to interpret these repeated expressions of support for women? Why did consecutive conferences feel the need to keep re-iterating their backing for women's equality? What was actually taking place – or not taking place – across workplaces in Britain?

The Buses Again

There were anxieties about relatively deteriorating wages amongst London bus workers, as the first section of this chapter has already outlined in relation to racial discrimination. There were fears that management was trying to introduce cheap labour (as in the case of the establishment of their recruitment office in Barbados) thereby depressing wages, rather than responding to trade unionists' campaigns for improvements. As a leading bus worker involved in campaigning on wages and conditions commented in relation to a subsequent campaign; 'We felt it morally wrong that London Transport should scour the world for competing labour for the peanuts they were paying, and that it was not a way to

26 MRC MSS.126/TG/1887/12. Minutes and Record of the 12th Biennial Delegate Conference, 1947.

Further Examples from the Print Industry

Whilst married women did work in the print industry, their opportunities were restricted, limitations that were generally accepted as the norm in the post-war period. Although women did not necessarily have to leave their jobs when they married, this was often the case, especially in the firms that paid the better wages. Married women only worked for 'pin money', it was widely believed. So, they didn't need the better paid jobs which should be reserved for women on their own. This view was very generally accepted at the time, amongst women as well as men. And this applied to women who had been doing 'men's jobs' – e.g. better paid jobs, such as guillotining, during the Second World War. After the war when the men returned from the forces, women generally had to leave these jobs.

Jobs were typically defined by gender in any case – there were men's jobs and women's jobs. And it was very unusual for women to get apprenticeships. Marie Bucksey (nee Thompson), one of the leading women trade unionists from the print industry (introduced in Chapter 2), was one of the very few women who ever managed to get indenture papers in the post-war period. Only boys would be trained as apprentices for 'craft' jobs; young women were classed as 'learners' with correspondingly restricted job opportunities as a result. When a group of women at a meeting were invited to put up their hands if they had indenture papers, Marie was the only one to do so. 'Blimey, Marie, I didn't know you had false teeth' someone commented! (Interview with Marie Bucksey, conducted by the author, 29 July, 2020) It may have been a joke, but a woman indentured as an apprentice was almost unknown.

This segregation between men and women's jobs was re-enforced by the Factory Act which laid down particular specifications about what women and youths were allowed to do as regards working hours. This was supposed to be for their protection. But there were some serious disadvantages as a result, including restrictions on access to night work. Not all women wanted to do night work. But some did, especially given that the men were managing to get paid for a full night's shift, even when they were working far less than that. Some women wanted a slice of the action here.

The confidence that women gained from the 1959 strike subsequently strengthened their resolve to challenge such restrictions. But job segregation continued in other ways for many years to come. Women in General Print only got into production areas in national newspapers after the amalgamation of the London branches in 1987, for instance.

Women in the print industry had also been organised in a separate Women's Branch of the union in London. After the Women's Branch amalgamated with the London Central Branch (the 'men's' branch) Ivy Smith became joint chair, successfully presiding over the first joint branch delegate meeting with the men in 1987 (despite an initial challenge from a disaffected man, calling to 'get that woman off the platform') (Interview with Marie Bucksey, conducted by the author, 29 July, 2020).

The women were often better informed and very effective in the union, they explained. And they needed to be, given the challenges that they had had to face. It was not only the employers that had been the problem. They had also faced problems from some of the men, although there were also men who were prepared to take a stand to support them. For instance, when Ivy had faced that call to 'get that woman off the platform' she had been supported by Ted Chard amongst other male members of the committee.

solve the problem', going on to explain: 'We were against cheap labour. We didn't care who took the job or what colour they were'. Still he did recognise that 'There were some who were anti-immigrant', even if they were in the minority in the union.[27]

There were parallels with bus workers' attitudes towards women working as bus conductors in London Transport. In 1950 a local conference agreed to the principle of having women employed as bus conductors, only for this to be rescinded, nine days later, at a mass meeting organised by the Dalston branch in East London. The meeting passed a resolution to let the GEC and their trade group representatives know that they had lost the men's confidence, pressing for a ban on overtime and the 'rescinding of the GEC agreement with LTE (London Transport Executive) along the lines of the slogan "one woman in, all out"'. Three days later more than 13,000 drivers and conductors from 14 garages and several tram and trolleybus depots were on strike over the issue of women conductors. The strike lasted for five days.[28]

This industrial action took place against the background of rank-and-file frustrations with the T&G's leadership under Deakin, frustrations that have already been outlined in Chapter 2. Rank-and-file activists' frustrations with management's attempts to undermine their claims were only too understandable as well. Small wonder that there was anger in response to management's divisive strategies. But that still leaves the problem of sexism amongst rank-and-file members of the T&G; however explicable, this could hardly be considered justifiable as a trade union response.

27 Ken Fuller, *Radical Aristocrats: London Busworkers from the 1880s to the 1980s* (Ishi Press, 2011), p.208.
28 Fuller, *Radical Aristocrats*.

Conclusions

As it has already been suggested, there were parallels as well as differences between these struggles for equalities in post-war Britain. Governments expressed varying degrees of ambivalence when it came to women's equalities, just as they had expressed varying degrees of ambivalence about migration and race. Labour shortages needed to be filled. But there were deep prejudices to be confronted when it came to the question of who should fill these gaps, and on what terms and conditions.

The Conservatives were far less reticent when it came to expressing their prejudices. But Labour ministers have come in for criticism too – and rightly so, the evidence suggests. These criticisms applied to some of their approaches to migration and racial discrimination. And there were criticisms to be applied to their reticence when it came to implementing equal pay provisions for equal work for women, along with their failures to maintain the services that had enabled women to work in wartime, nurseries, nursery classes, childcare centres and civic canteens.

The T&G has been described as having much to be proud of, in contrast. The record of biennial conference decisions bears this out. The T&G was clearly opposed to racial discrimination in principle, just as the union was opposed to discrimination against women in terms of the issue of equal pay for equal work. But these policy positions only represented one part of the story. The reality was that there were struggles to be waged within the T&G on both fronts. There were battles against racism, just as there were struggles against attempts to exclude women from particular categories of jobs, let alone to encourage them to apply for key positions within the T&G itself.

There were differences too, and varying responses within the T&G, according to different areas and trades. But there were also interconnections in terms of the underlying factors involved. There were employers who were only too happy to take advantage of differences within the labour force. There were governments that were only too ready to allow Britain's efforts to achieve economic recovery to be borne disproportionately by some rather than others, whether these were migrant workers or women workers who were being expected to bear these disproportionate burdens, or both. And there were ideological factors involved, legacies of Empire that were being used to justify more contemporary forms of discrimination, as Beveridge's view of the proper role of mothers so clearly indicated, their vital work in 'ensuring the adequate continuance of the British Race and of British Ideals in the world'.[29]

The extent to which such attitudes have changed remains a question for further discussion. Some attitudes have changed of course, as a result

---

29 Quoted in Wilson, *Women and the Welfare State*, p.150.

of collective struggles, including many attitudes about women's equality in the workplace. But other attitudes would seem to be particularly resistant to change. Women still face discrimination at work just as they still face harassment and domestic violence more generally. And anti-Semitism continues to be a challenge, along with racism, xenophobia and extreme forms of nationalism in Britain, as elsewhere. A recent survey (2019) found that a third of people in UK believed that Britain's colonies were better off for being part of the Empire, in fact, a higher proportion than in any other major former colonial power, it seems.[30] Britons were also more likely to say that they would like their country to have an Empire still, compared with people in France, Italy, Spain, the Netherlands, Belgium, Germany or Japan. What, if anything might this tell us about the continuing strength of nationalist sentiments – including xenophobic and racist sentiments? Were most Britons not aware of their country's role in the slave trade, critics wondered, let alone aware of the contributions that Africans and other colonised peoples have made to this country? There are so many challenges for the trade union movement today.

Questions for Discussion: Chapter 4

- How would you summarise the similarities between the struggles for women's equalities and racial equalities within the T&G?

- How would you summarise the differences?

- How relevant do you think it is for trade unionists to have a critical understanding of Britain's colonial past?

---

30 Robert Booth, 'UK more nostalgic for empire than other ex-colonial powers', *The Guardian* (2020), https://www.theguardian.com/world/2020/mar/11/uk-more-nostalgic-for-empire-than-other-ex-colonial-powers.

5

Using Education to Build the Union, 1945–1960

Introduction: Different Approaches to Workers' Education and Training over Time

Previous chapters have explored a range of T&G policies in the post-war period, comparing the union's approaches under the contrasting leaderships of Arthur Deakin and Frank Cousins. These differences ran through their very different approaches to industrial relations and trade union democracy, here in Britain, just as they ran through their very different approaches to international relations and solidarity with movements for colonial freedom in the context of the Cold War. Such differences of perspective could be traced throughout the union at every level, from the shop floor upwards, as struggles for equalities illustrated in the preceding chapter. No surprises then to find that there were differences of view about the purposes of education and training within the T&G, along with differences of view about the most appropriate educational methods to be applied.

The trade union and labour movement has a history of debates about the role of education more generally, dating back over the past century and even beyond. Was education to be primarily concerned with its utility, providing workers with the knowledge and skills that they needed in order to cope with rapid economic and social change? This was what the Mechanics Institutes that were established in the nineteenth century set out to achieve. But this approach didn't seem to include strategies for empowering workers to change the existing economic order, as Engels, amongst other critics, had argued. Conversely then, should education be about promoting what has been termed 'really useful knowledge'. This was what the corresponding societies, socialist Sunday schools, co-operative societies and Chartists aimed to provide, knowledge to enable people to analyse their situations in order to promote democratic forms of change, working for social justice from the bottom up. This was the position advocated by the London & Provincial Union of Licensed Vehicle Workers (which subsequently became part of T&G in 1922) at its 1917 Annual Delegate Meeting, for instance, instructing the EC to provide resources for education in this wider sense.

These debates continued into the twentieth century. There were parallels with the tensions that emerged between major adult education providers, Ruskin College, Oxford (founded in 1899), the Workers' Educational Association (WEA) (founded in 1903) and the National Council of Labour Colleges (NCLC). This third provider was established precisely because of these differences, emerging from a split at Ruskin in the wake of a student strike which had taken place back in 1909. There is not the space here for more than a very brief outline of these debates to identify the key areas of contention.

In summary, the Ruskin strike had centred around the question of whether the college's role should be to equip its students to challenge the existing social order and work to transform it – or to prepare students to function within the limitations set by existing social relations, preparing future leaders to operate effectively within the status quo, as the Marxist educationalist Brian Simon has summarised this dilemma.[1] There were also related debates about the desirability – or otherwise – of links with the University of Oxford. Critics were suspicious of university experts, concerned about courses becoming too academic, too distant from the issues of more immediate concern to trade unionist and labour activists. Others, conversely, argued that the NCLC's alternative wasn't education at all, however, merely class-war propaganda.

There were differences too when it came to the most appropriate teaching methods. The NCLC criticised the WEA tradition – and Ruskin – for being too liberal, committed to putting both sides of the argument, rather than presenting a clear set of prescriptions, based upon a Marxist analysis of the issues in question. And the NCLC was criticised in its turn, for indoctrinating its students rather than providing student-led approaches to learning, promoting critical thinking and active student engagement. Methods and purposes don't necessarily fit together that neatly then. 'Progressive' teaching methods can be applied within relatively limited education programmes, just as more 'traditional' methods can be applied for wider educational ends, as will be suggested subsequently, in the context of more recent T&G experiences.

In addition, there have been differences of view about the most appropriate sources of funding, particularly the vexed question of state funding. To what extent would state funding limit the options in terms of what was to be taught, a question that had been hotly debated in the first part of the twentieth century. This has re-emerged as an issue of

---

1 Brian Simon, *The Search for Enlightenment: The Working Class and Adult Education in the Twentieth Century* (NIACE, 1992).

concern more recently, with the growth of state funding from the 1960s, with considerable effects on trade union education as a result. By the end of the 1970s, politics had been virtually eliminated from the curriculum, as a result of what has been described as this 'Faustian pact', it has been argued.[2] The following volume explores these questions in further detail.

At the end of the day, however, educational impacts would seem to be inherently unpredictable, whatever the intentions of the providers in question. The title of John Fisher's history of T&G education, *Bread on the Waters*, makes precisely this point. It was (perhaps ironically) Arthur Deakin who had used this phrase to refer to spending the union's money on education. This was, he said, like 'bread cast upon the waters'.[3] Although Arthur Deakin had his own agendas for education in the T&G, he was evidently only too aware of the unpredictability of the outcomes. Learners would respond in their own ways, whatever the intentions of the providers.

The Background to T&G's Approaches to Education and Training in the Post-War Period

So how did these debates relate to the history of education and training within the T&G? Ever since its foundation in 1922, the T&G had involved itself in providing education for its active members. Before the war, however, most of this education had been provided as a benefit to members who might have missed out on schooling or as a way of broadening their knowledge, particularly in areas like politics and economics. Education had been mainly provided by outside bodies using adult education tutors, especially those from the WEA and the NCLC – with their varying traditions and approaches. The Labour Party and Communist Party had also run schools which T&G members attended.

The union's own emphasis had been on its correspondence course. This focused on providing information about the union's formal structures, together with basic literacy and numeracy skills. Although this educational provision indirectly strengthened and benefited the union, there was no direct link between education and building the T&G's organisation per se, however.

After the war, the direction and objectives of the union's education provision changed radically, becoming much more integrated into its organising objectives. There was particular emphasis on training to develop the newly active heart of the union in the workplace – its growing body of shop stewards.

2 M. McGrath, 'Backstory: A Unite Approach to Political Education' in Mike Seal (ed.), *Trade Union Education* (New Internationalist, 2017), pp.100–114, p.101.

3 Fisher, *Bread on the Waters*, p.9.

It may seem paradoxical that the general secretary, Arthur Deakin, comes out of this particular part of the T&G's story as a genuine champion of T&G education. So why was this? Education could be envisaged as a site of the class struggle after all, promoting critical consciousness, building the critical understanding that would be needed for more effective activism from the grassroots upwards. This could be described as education for liberation as the introduction to this chapter has already outlined, with reference to the writings of Paulo Freire. Yet here was Arthur Deakin championing education, the very same Arthur Deakin who has already emerged from previous chapters as the scourge of the Left, enthusiastically embracing the crusade against communism, driving through the 1949 biennial conference resolution banning communists from holding office in the union.

The reality was less paradoxical by far, however. Education could also be promoted for very different agendas, as the introduction to this chapter has also pointed out. Arthur Deakin was quite comfortable with the type of education programme that essentially focused on the industrial role of the union. Far from inciting radicalism, in fact, this type of education could have the opposite effects, he believed, producing better educated members who would more readily reject 'extremism' of whatever kind. So this was the rationale, helping to explain why Deakin gave his full support to the expansion and refocusing of the union's education programme.

There were, in addition, further reasons for Deakin's enthusiastic support for the development of T&G's educational programme. There was increasing interest in the development of new approaches to management at the time, drawing on US strategies to increase productivity in the post-war period. British employers were beginning to apply techniques such as time and motion studies and job evaluations in parallel. Clearly shop stewards needed training in these approaches if they were to support their members most effectively. So the T&G needed to provide the courses that they needed – never mind Deakin's distinctly negative attitudes towards shop stewards – in the context of their roles in unofficial stoppages. Key figures developing these courses were Ellen McCullough (already introduced in the previous chapter) and Tony Corfield, who led the move towards more practical, workplace-related educational methods.

The T&G's Education Programmes Develop in the Post-War Period

Immediately after the war, the correspondence course continued. Specially tailored trade union courses were also established at the London School of Economics and at the TUC. But times were changing and new demands being made. And the balance of educational provision was beginning to shift in response.

Discussions on the organisation and direction of post-war trade union education had already been taking place within the union from 1944

Ellen Mccullough: Key Figure in T&G Education at This Time

One of the key figures in developing the education programme at this time was Ellen McCullough, who led or influenced the union's education programme throughout the whole period. Ellen McCullough has already been introduced in the previous chapter as one of the most prominent women in the T&G at this time. She had been a clerk in the Workers' Union since 1925 when she was 16 years old.

She had helped to form the Hendon branch of the WEA and had been active in the Labour Party in North London. In 1933 she had won the Mary McArthur scholarship for working women, for the University of London Diploma in Public Administration and Sociology. She had also attended the first ILO/WEA summer school in Geneva in 1934, writing a report on this from a student's point of view. She cut her teeth in the union's education programme whilst developing the correspondence course, and with some interruptions, she was to remain in charge of T&G education throughout the 1940s, 1950s and 1960s, never breaking her links with the WEA

onwards. In May of that year, the Education Committee had received a detailed paper, written by Ellen McCullough, entitled *Memorandum on the Question of Post-War Policy in Relation to Workers' Education*. This sought to link the T&G's education programme to the industrial work of the union more closely, using officials rather than academic tutors as providers, as the following quotation explains: 'For instance, a course of lectures, or a class, on the machinery of collective bargaining would be greatly assisted by the attendance at one of its sessions of a man [*sic*] with wide first-hand experience of the way in which JICs and statutory bodies work'.[4] This paper led the way in reorienting the union's education provision.

Developing Shop Stewards' Education

Ellen McCullogh recognised the problem that the pattern of day and weekend schools lacked any real industrial focus, and that they were not part of any strategic plan for the development of an increasingly important element within the union – the shop steward. The number of

---

4 Ellen McCullough, *Memorandum on the Question of Post-War Policy in Relation to Workers' Education*, quoted in Fisher, *Bread on the Waters*.

shop stewards had increased as had their influence immediately before and during the war, encouraged by younger and more innovative officials. If T&G education was to remain a central part of the union's organising activity, then it would need to come to terms with this reality. The union would also need to extend the earlier focus of the correspondence course and day schools, which were primarily about understanding the structure and function of the union as an organisation, together with some coverage of wider political and economic issues. The T&G needed to introduce courses that were much more directly relevant to the shop stewards' agendas and roles in the workplace.

There was also pressure from within the union. Some of the union's trade groups had started to make demands for courses on issues such as 'Time and Motion Study' and 'Scientific Management' as these approaches to management were being brought in via the new industries, often, if not always, from the US. This more systematic, industry-oriented approach to trade union education was also given a boost from two other directions. Firstly, some of the newly nationalised industries like port transport and road haulage began trade union and/or joint union-management training around industrial relations issues within these industries. Secondly, targeted shop stewards' training had already been strongly promoted by the Training Within Industry (TWI) initiative. This system had been introduced from the US during the war by Ernest Bevin as part of the drive to increase productivity through joint production techniques. It was primarily aimed at supervisors and foremen to assist them in instructing others and increasing productivity. By mid-1945, the Ministry of Labour claimed to have trained over 10,000 supervisors. The scheme was then extended to residential courses at universities for what would now be called personnel or human resource managers. But what about the rest of the labour force?

After the war, TWI was in fact extended to shop stewards at a limited number of technical colleges, primarily Leicester, Nottingham and Birmingham. TWI included many of the educational methods which we would now recognise as being fundamental in trade union education; targeted objectives and measured outcomes; role play and other active learning techniques, team-teaching and interactive course materials. It also included training in leadership and in improving working methods, along with the 'job safety' programme, which focused on accident prevention. In particular, it included the military 'drill' approach to handling industrial relations problems, summarised as follows:

1) Get the facts

2) Weigh and decide

3) Take action, and

4) Check results.

Tony Corfield (1920–2011): Another Key Figure in T&G Education at This Time

Tony Corfield went to Oxford in 1938, where his tutor had an association with Ruskin College, a link which introduced him to trade union education. He was called up into the army in 1940, where he was involved in training for the Parachute Regiment as a weapons training officer. This was a formative experience that he drew upon, when returning to civilian life in 1947. As he himself explained:

'My main contribution to trade union education was to realise that it was based on method and the achievement of practical ends [...] I brought the practical stuff in [...]. I learned a lot from the army, particularly from the German Army method of education and training'. The important thing was logic, order and measured outcomes. 'What is your job, what is your purpose?' 'Trade union education should be very close to drill' (See Tony Corfield and Ellen McCullough, *Trade Union Branch Officers Manual* (Chapman and Hall, 1964), p.106–107).

Tony Corfield was education officer for the T&G between 1950 and 1968, serving under both Arthur Deakin and Frank Cousins as general secretaries. As education officer he pioneered programmes for shop stewards featuring negotiation skills, public speaking and the law. He left the T&G in 1968, going on to become the social studies director for the WEA. His last post was as principal of Fircroft College of Adult Education in Birmingham, from 1971 to 1976. He died at the age of 91 in 2011.

This 'drill' approach was to be central to the T&G's approach to shop stewards' education throughout this period and beyond, developed and promoted by Tony Corfield amongst others. This was a world away from the university/liberal education methods that had been used before the war in trade union education.

The 1949 Biennial Delegate Conference (BDC) and the First Summer Schools

These new developments were reflected in debates on education in the union at the time. Concerns about them came to a head at the 1949 BDC. For this biennial conference Ellen McCullough and Arthur Deakin prepared a comprehensive statement on the future of education within the union. Ellen McCullough was then challenged about the expenditure that this would incur. She was also challenged about the fact that out of a total membership of 1,323,000, only 1,500 members had taken part in education. How could this represent value for money? But together she and the general secretary were able to win the conference over with their comprehensive proposals, which were then taken to the GEC. At its November 1949 meeting, as a result the proposals were accepted on the basis of an overall allocation of £25,000 (£500,000 at today's values) per annum to meet the cost of the new scheme. Having agreement to devote such significant resources to education within the T& was a massive step forward.

The union's interests in the field of adult education were set out as threefold:

1) General education of a liberal kind, including the use of language, economics, history, philosophy, psychology and sociology

2) Education and training for specifically trade union purposes, including the education of branch officers and workshop representatives

3) Education in connection with the industries in which our members are engaged, including technical training and training for management.

Bearing these principles in mind, the following proposals were made, proposals which were to shape the union's education programme for a generation. First of all, every area was encouraged to consider the extent to which the TWI could be adapted to their use. Officers trained by TWI were then to be encouraged to hold two-day courses for shop stewards in their own localities and trades. The union was to meet the full cost of these courses by paying the members attending them as if they were on union business – including payment for 'loss of time'. Further training (for two full weeks at one of the technical colleges that were offering TWI) was to be offered to those completing the first level course. And most significantly, the union was to introduce summer schools, organised by the WEA for the union, for branch chairmen, [sic] branch secretaries and for 'other branch officers' (meaning shop stewards who were not officially recognised in the T&G rulebook).

The New Residential Schools

It was recognised that there was a difference between a TWI-based course for supervisors and a TWI-based course for shop stewards. The main difference, though, was not so much methodological or content wise (in the areas of industrial relations that were to be covered by these courses). Rather the difference has been described as being essentially ideological.

The wartime pattern of joint production committees – into which TWI had fitted so well – had broken down by the early 1950s. So, there was a need to reinforce the independent role of trade unions in general along with reinforcing the role of the shop steward more particularly.

The other – very significant – innovation was to move the residential schools away from the more open, philosophical discussions that had been typical of the pre-war WEA. Rather the move was towards the incorporation of the 'drill' approach of TWI. There were T&G officials and a new generation of adult education tutors who made sure that these new methods were central to the approach that was adopted at these residential schools. During 1952, the *TGWU Shop Stewards' Handbook* was prepared for circulation throughout the union. This was launched in early 1953.

There was clearly a need to employ at least one new member of staff who was committed to this new focus on shop stewards and was conversant with the new active-learning and TWI-based teaching methods. Ellen McCullough's choice was Tony Corfield, who had gained experience of such methods during the war, as has already been explained. Tony Corfield became a key figure in the development of T&G education as a result.

The key to understanding Corfield's approach is the word *drill*. Building from his army experiences, he was unashamedly committed to a structured and systematic approach to education, with predetermined methods and outcomes. He was convinced that this was more suitable for T&G students than the more traditional WEA 'liberal' approach. TWI suited him perfectly. This approach became the norm within the union from the early 1950s. It also became the basis of the TUC courses from 1964 onwards and for the education programmes of most, if not all, individual unions subsequently.

Tony Corfield's approach fitted extremely well with Deakin's wider agendas too. This was about a very practical view of trade union education, enhancing trade unionists' effectiveness, as negotiators, addressing issues of pay and conditions including health and safety. However essential such knowledge and skills most clearly were, this was a very limited view of the role of the trade union and labour movement more generally though. What about the contributions that political education could also make towards trade union and labour movement's agendas for longer-term change?

This was not about making choices between either one or the other of course. Subsequent general secretaries (including Jack Jones) shared Arthur Deakin's commitment to the more practical aspects of trade union education. As Jack Jones's preface to John Fisher's history of T&G education between 1922 and 2000 explains, 'the need for a strong and effective educational aspect has been increasingly recognised'. 'This service', he continued, 'strengthens our efforts to effectively represent our needs and aspirations in the industrial field, and to successfully represent our fellow workers and ourselves [...] This work has grown and has become

Figure 8: Jack Jones

an essential part of the effective representation of members' needs'.[5] But this preface concluded with allusions to the wider goals of the trade union and labour movement as well. 'Knowledge leads to influence' Jack Jones reflected, part of the wider 'march forward of a successful trade union'.[6]

But this is to jump ahead, raising wider issues of relevance for trade union education for the future. Back in 1953, there were more immediate issues of concern for the education department. The first one was to find a settled home for the T&G's summer school programme. The second was to work out what needed to be organised for the 'follow-on' students who had passed through the summer schools and were therefore looking for a more advanced level of study. This marked the earliest recognition that there was a case for a system of progression within T&G education, a need that grew as more students entered the system.

By the end of 1952, Ellen McCullough had already addressed the first of these concerns, i.e. to find a settled home for the summer schools. This involved making contact with the governors of the Royal Agricultural

5 Jones, *Union Man*, p.6.
6 Fisher, *Bread on the Waters*, p.6.

Figure 9: Cirencester event

College at Cirencester. The plan for 1953 was to book this college for the whole of August, for residential schools for approximately 250 students. These students would each be selected for a one-week course, chosen on the basis of recommendations from their regional secretaries.

The first Cirencester summer school was held from 1–29 August 1953. Tutors were a mixture of academics who were sympathetic to the union, along with T&G officials who were to lead on specialist subjects. By 1955 the union had settled into the pattern of using Cirencester for all its national summer schools. This pattern remained the same into the 1980s, and became the core of the union's link between education and organising.

The programme included a communications course which looked at statistics and procedures, rules of debate, motions, and letter writing; a branch chairman's course which looked at chairing meetings; and a committeemen [sic] delegates' course which again looked at procedures, motions and branch activities. The programme also included a branch secretaries' course which covered agendas, letter writing, minutes and so on, and a shop stewards' course which looked at grievance procedures, and practical exercises. There were, in addition, two more theoretical elements to the programme. One focused on the governance of trade unions, whilst the other was a follow-on course for students who had already completed a summer school course the previous year, moving on to explore wider economic and wage policy issues.

In summary then, it was during the period from 1950 to 1956 that the union established the prototype of its national members' school. This became the training-ground for several generations of T&G activists and full-time officials. The system had evolved from TWI and the experiences of a number of the key tutor-organisers, with its main focus on practical industrial problems. Coupled with active learning methods, the system was seen to suit T&G activists perfectly.[7] The courses never lost their popularity apparently, becoming an 'institution', continuing as a central feature of the T&G's education programme for decades. It was only in the 1980s and 1990s that regional educational programmes overtook them in terms of the numbers of courses and students involved, as subsequent volumes will go on to explain.

Methods and Objectives in the Post-War Period

The significance of the TWI scheme was not only that it provided a new focus on shop stewards and workplace relations as central to the union's education mission. The TWI scheme was also the vehicle for the introduction of new active learning methods, such as role play and other participative techniques. The significance of this revolution in methodology was fully recognised at the time, as was the contrast which these methods provided as compared with the pre-war approaches of both the NCLC and the WEA. Most trade union education in the earlier period had been based on the lecture followed by a question-and-answer session for the participants. This report from *The Record* in 1948 gives a flavour of the traditional type of school provided by bodies like the WEA and university extramural departments:

> Some 70 students were in residence. An international air pervaded the school. There was Walter Stude a Swiss; a schoolmaster from Hanover and his three German compatriots, one a Fraulein flown straight from Berlin; our dark brothers [*sic*] from the West Indies, with much knowledge of racial discrimination; Vernon, the Ceylonese; Jack and a friend from Nigeria – Jack knew a thing or two about ground nuts. Chicago University as well as Toronto were worthily represented by adept and voluble individuals; 'The Vivacious Mademoiselle' was an asset, and lastly but by no means least, was the lady from Jerusalem and the disciples of Marx and Engels.[8]

This sounds admirably internationalist, with the potential for exploring many of the issues that have already been raised in the previous chapter,

7 Fisher, *Bread on the Waters*.
8 *The Record*, September 1948, p.73.

linking equalities struggles across national boundaries. But most of the new shop stewards who were now building the union did not see this as so relevant to their role in the same way. They had more specific concerns to examine. And they appreciated having the opportunity to explore them in far less traditional ways.

By the time that the Cirencester summer schools had become established then, teaching methods had been completely changed as a result of the different approaches that had been developed by Tony Corfield's generation of tutors. The summer schools used WEA tutors who were essentially younger university lecturers in the 'extramural' tradition, many of whom had a specific political commitment to trade unionism along with a willingness to work in very different ways. The focus was upon more practical issues and outcomes.

The syllabus was in two sections; the morning consisted of training in practical skills such as report-making, note-taking and representation. In the afternoon there were sessions concerned with the union's wider roles and responsibilities in relation to employers, the Labour Party and the Labour movement. There was documentation to provide back-up for each section of the course. And there was particular emphasis on the use of practical activities such as role-plays and exercises in public speaking – both indoors and outdoors – as well as sessions on issues such as how to organise branch meetings, including exercises on how to deal with resolutions.

Tony Corfield also developed training manuals. As he himself explained: 'The essence of the manuals is that the training should be on the principle of learning by doing. The centre of interest and activity is switched away from the platform speaker and into the body of the audience'.[9] These manuals covered areas such as making branch policy, the wider links between the union and the Labour Party, the work of the shop steward and the legal responsibility of branch officers. By the mid-1960s, when the TUC introduced its standardised shop stewards' course (based on the Swedish Study Circles' active learning methods) T&G students had long been familiar with this approach to trade union education.

The Debate on Longer Courses

By the mid-1950s, the basic pattern of the union's education programme was to use the home study course as the first stage. Students would then be encouraged to attend the summer school, where they would be trained using the teaching manuals. After that, they could attend the follow-on course, which was usually, although not always, organised at Cirencester.

9 Interview with Tony Corfield, 26 March 1998, in Fisher, *Bread on the Waters*.

But this still left the question of the role of longer courses. How if at all, were these to fit into the T&G's approach overall?

Tony Corfield's own firm rejection of what he termed vague academic methods has already been emphasised in relation to the provision of short courses. But he was not opposed to the provision of longer study-based courses per se. On the contrary, in fact, he had been keen to introduce some longer courses including the 'Busmen's Long Course' at Transport House, for example. This was a three-year series of classes which included more in the way of academic requirements. The students all had to write essays regularly, for instance.

The inaugural meeting of this series of tutorial classes was held on 2 November 1953, with 50 students in attendance. The course covered subjects such as the functions and structure of trade unions, economic problems and trade unions and politics. In order to tailor this long course to meet the needs of shift workers, it was decided that the class would meet on Tuesday mornings and then again on Tuesday evenings. Identical classes were given at both sessions on each day so that students on shift work could attend at least one of them. This was a popular offering. By 1956, the course was becoming oversubscribed, with too many students turning up for the new classes. Despite the popularity of these longer forms of more academic study, they attracted some questioning amongst the membership more widely though. Was it really worth spending so much on these longer courses? Were they actually relevant?

Similar arguments had already been raised in relation to the provision of scholarships for T&G students to gain access to higher education through studying at Ruskin and elsewhere. These scholarships had only represented a very small proportion of educational spending. But they provoked considerable debate, with critics pointing to the fact that some graduates left the union once they had obtained their qualifications. Was this value for money from the union's point of view? It was Frank Cousins himself who intervened on this occasion, as follows: 'As to those who use the LSE and Ruskin College as a jumping-ground as betterment for themselves, let us remember the others who went to those places and used them as a medium to help others. Let us not get it out of perspective'.[10]

Keen to deflect any such criticisms in advance of the biennial conference in 1959, however, the GEC made it plain that 'future union educational policy was to be primarily based upon a desire that there should be a greater emphasis on the development of a service more widely related to the internal needs of the membership'.[11] It was also proposed that the regions should be more systematic in their approach to educational provision, relating this to the needs of the membership more closely too.

10 Fisher, *Bread on the Waters* p.122.
11 GEC, March 3rd, 1959. Minute No. 134. p.29.

But regional schools could also deal with larger issues, it was conceded, including issues such as economic development, wages and productivity, current developments in union organisation and the relationship between the trade union movement and politics, more generally.

Day Release: Towards Paid Educational Leave

One further educational development of longer-term significance during this period was the growth of day release. There had already been some history of day release within the T&G, although the numbers had been relatively small. But Jack Jones had laid the groundwork for the future expansion of day release on a significant scale during his time as regional secretary in the Midlands. In his autobiography Jack Jones recounts the story as follows. Following the strikes in the Birmingham and Oxford BMC plants (already outlined in Chapter 2) he sought an interview with management – George Harriman – suggesting that it was about time that management adopted a less confrontational approach towards shop stewards. If stewards and active members were driven underground this could be more damaging to the Corporation in the long run, he pointed out.

'Harriman was no pushover' Jack Jones explained, 'he was thick-skinned and sarcastic, but he listened when I turned the discussion to the need for shop stewards' education and training. My argument was that it was no use his complaining about the conduct of stewards if he was not prepared to help in training them'. Jack Jones went on to point out that this would have to be done during working hours, adding that 'it would raise the status of the stewards if they were allowed time off from work, with the management paying their wages for the periods concerned'. 'I knew that Harriman would not swallow the idea of the union alone doing the training', he continued, 'so I proposed that the tuition should be paid for by the union but undertaken by the extramural department of Birmingham University'. Harriman was still suspicious, but Jack Jones pressed the point, adding that 'the chief man in the extra-mural department is Mr Parker, who is a friend of the Royal Family, so you can be sure of his impartiality'. This seemed to clinch the argument!

As Jack Jones concluded, reflecting on the significance of this development, 'From little acorns big oaks grow; from that first agreement grew the whole process of shop stewards' training in works' time throughout the Midlands, and the whole country for that matter'.[12]

12 Jones, *Union Man*, p.147.

In Summary

Throughout the immediate post-war years, student numbers rose in response to the significant extensions of the union's educational facilities. An analysis of T&G students in 1948–1949 showed that 1,583 students were enrolled for correspondence courses and that a total of 630 students had attended day and weekend schools, including 450 on the union's own schools. By the early 1950s, the department was claiming annual student numbers of around 10,000. This was partly due to an extremely inclusive way of counting students attending WEA, NCLC and similar external bodies.

These numbers also treated each student place as a 'new' student, involving some double counting (when students were attending more than one course). Nevertheless, these increases in student numbers were still impressive. In 1950, for example, the department claimed a total number of 10,652 students, including 2,000 on correspondence courses with Ruskin and the NCLC, 2,500 on the T&G correspondence course, 229 with summer school scholarships, 51 at the T&G summer school, 2,500 attending WEA or NCLC day and weekend schools, 3,000 on T&G day and weekend schools, 62 on TUC training courses, 17 full-time scholarships, 10 at the LSE, 249 attending special weekend schools for shop stewards, 24 shop stewards training in Leicester on the TWI long course, and 10 attending a shop stewards' evening course in Cardiff.

TGWU Student Numbers 1951–1954 and 1955–1956

Year	Total students	Short courses	B/O students*
1951–1952	19,026	1,983	1,957
1953–1954	19,484	3,711	2,878
1955–1956	19,154	2,315	3,185

Source: TGWU Education Department Reports, taken from Fisher, *Bread on the Waters*, p.128.
* Branch officers course students

In 1957 the total number of students for the year was 8,683, which was 200 less than 1956. The figures for one or two-week courses, however, had actually increased because of the emphasis on attendance at the union's own training courses and the national summer schools. Short course students in 1957 were 4,934, correspondence students 3,285, students on courses lasting one or two weeks, 550. In any event these are impressive numbers, showing the increasingly comprehensive nature of the T&G's education programme by the time that Frank Cousins became general secretary. Frank Cousins continued to support the programme during his time as general secretary despite the costs involved.[13]

The great achievement of the immediate post-war period was the introduction and consolidation of the branch officers' summer schools based on active learning methods. As the 1960s evolved, these began to be equalled in importance by local initiatives based on day release, reaching a climax when the next general secretary, Jack Jones, established the appointment of a regional education officer (REO) in every region of the union. But these developments are for the following volume.

This particular period marked what has been described as one of the most consistently creative periods in the history of the union's education programme then, reflecting the shift from the more bureaucratic, staid union of Bevin and Deakin to the more open, left-leaning T&G of Frank Cousins and Jack Jones. The key industrial issues of the period were the development of plant and company bargaining and the key roles that were played in this process by shop stewards. The T&G's education programme played a vital part in these developments through the summer schools and through the focus on training branch officers and shop stewards' skills in the skills that they required to address these changes effectively. This approach was central to the thinking of Tony Corfield, Ellen McCullough and other supportive officers, tutors and organisers, as this chapter has already described. The hard work of the late 1940s and 1950s put the T&G in a strong position to take advantage of even more radical changes with the opportunities and challenges of the 1960s, the period which saw the rise of Jack Jones, the spread of day release and the beginning of the TUC shop stewards' education scheme.

Conclusions

This had indeed been a remarkable period in terms of the development of education and training within the T&G. There were major implications for the union's strengths for the future. These developments were to be particularly significant at shop-floor level, as shop stewards were enabled to gain the knowledge and skills that they required, engaging in bargaining over wages and conditions on a plant by plant basis. The shop stewards' movement was strengthened as a result, enabling shop stewards to take on the new management techniques that were being imported from the US more effectively, in a changing industrial context.

Education and training developments had particularly important potential too, in terms of the promotion of equalities agendas, even if

---

13 For further information on Cousin's support for the programme see Fisher, *Bread on the Waters*.

these were still seriously underdeveloped. Women were demanding more opportunities for education and training as the previous chapter has already pointed out. How far these demands were being met is another question. There were major issues here for the future. As subsequent experiences were to go on demonstrate, education and training could enhance women's abilities to strengthen their positions within the union as well as within the workplace. And education and training for BAME members could also enable them to gain the knowledge and skills – along with the collective confidence – to challenge discrimination within the union as well as within the workplace and beyond.

This was also a period of significant change in terms of the introduction of different educational methods and approaches. The traditional format for adult education – involving lectures, followed by question-and-answer sessions and group discussions – was no longer predominant, with great emphasis upon more active forms of student-centred learning. These changes raise further questions in their turn, however, questions that relate back to the differing purposes of education and training more fundamentally. Was this only to focus on providing trade unionists with the practical knowledge and skills that they needed in order to represent their members' interests most effectively? Or should this also include opportunities to gain the economic, social and political understandings that they needed if they were to be better fitted 'for the responsibilities of membership of political, social and industrial organizations' as the celebrated educationalists, R. H. Tawney and Basil Yeaxlee had argued in their introduction to the *Report on Adult Education,* way back in 1919. Was this just about strengthening the trade union and labour movement's capacities for bargaining within the status quo of existing – and unequal – social relationships? Or was this also about education for social change, economic, social and political education for the longer term – Jack Jones's view, amongst others.

These were not simply questions about educational methodologies, as it has already been suggested. Active, student-centred learning methods could be used to promote students' understandings of the underlying causes of social inequalities and discrimination, just as such methods could be used within the confines of far more restricted agendas. And conversely, lecturers could find ways to stimulate critical thinking, too, even within the format of the traditional lecture. This takes the discussion back to the more fundamental questions that have already been raised in the introduction to this chapter, questions about the overall purposes of trade union education in the first place.

Reflecting on more recent approaches to political education in Unite, Mick McGrath has seen education as being part of the wider battle of ideas, a site of struggle 'in which reps are equipped to undertake their day-to-day organizational and representational functions along with developing their understanding of the economic order as a construct which operates in the interests of the few and to the detriment of the many'. This was about developing political class consciousness, he argued, drawing on the theoretical works of the Italian Marxist, Antonio Gramsci, along with the educational approaches that were developed by Paulo Freire, the progressive Brazilian adult educator.[14] There was a link here too with Paulo Freire's recognition of his debt to Gramsci's thinking about challenging the 'common sense' of existing – and unequal – social relations, building critical consciousness in the process.

But how to balance the need for political education of this type with the pressures associated with the provision of state funding for trade union education? Mick McGrath described the provision of the state funding from the 1960s as a Faustian pact, extending the provision of trade union education – but at the cost of disabling 'educators from engaging in political and economic analysis'.[15] How then could trade unions respond to such pressures, equipping their members with the necessary knowledge and skills whilst still developing members' wider understandings? These are questions for discussion in subsequent volumes – with the following questions for discussion in relation to this particular period more specifically.

---

14 McGrath, 'Backstory', p.103.
15 McGrath, 'Backstory', p.103.

Questions for Discussion: Chapter 5

- How far do you think that Arthur Deakin's support for the development of education in the T&G was consistent with his view of the role of trade unionism, more generally?

- To what extent did T&G's approach to education change during this period? Were there parallels with other changes of direction more generally during this period or not?

- How far did T&G's education programmes contribute to equalities agendas in this period?

- What might be the parallels – if any – with more recent strategies to go 'beyond functionalism' in the provision of education and training in the T&G?

6

Debates on Democracy
and Alternative Futures

This chapter starts by focusing on questions of democracy within the T&G, questions that were linked to very different approaches to the role of trade unions more generally. There were debates about centralisation versus democratisation during Deakin's time as general secretary, as he attempted to manage unofficial shop-floor militancy, as Chapter 2 has outlined. 'Whose side are you on?', trade unionists had asked of their leaderships in such contexts. Jack Jones himself took a very different approach, building on Cousins's achievements as general secretary, giving far more weight to rank-and-file involvement, building trade union democracy from the shop floor upwards. There were, in addition, debates about questions of equalities within the T&G. How were women's interests to be represented and with what forms of support? These issues have already emerged in Chapters 4 and 5.

Having explored these questions about representation within the T&G itself, the chapter moves on to focus on broader debates about what type of society the trade union and labour movement should be aiming to achieve for the future. And what, more specifically, should be the role of nationalisation – the issue that was central to battles for the soul of the Labour Party at the end of this period. Should there be further nationalisations as part of longer-term strategies to promote industrial democracy and socialism? Or should decisions about nationalisation have more restricted aims, only to be used as a tactic of last resort to return particular industries to profitability within the confines of existing social relations? These questions relate to wider debates about the nature of the interrelationships between capital, labour and the state, together with wider debates about equalities and social justice both in Britain and beyond on an international scale.

Different Approaches to Democracy Within the T&G

The structure that Bevin had bequeathed to the T&G has been described by the trade union historian Allen Hutt as being 'ingenious – combining a high degree of centralisation with a double division of its members, vertically by industrial groups and horizontally by areas'.[1] This structure had 'enabled this powerful body to be substantially dominated by its forceful general secretary, Mr Ernest Bevin', Hutt continued. This was the structure that Deakin inherited, a structure that broadly stood the test of time, as Andrew Murray explained in his history, *The T&G Story*.[2] Both industrial and regional structures were needed to take account of the diversity of conditions across a multiplicity of industries and geographical areas. This was a structure which 'allowed the T&G to act locally while thinking nationally or even globally'.[3]

There were inherent tensions, however. The union's structures were essentially democratic. But critics have pointed to significant gaps in the union's structures too. Reflecting on what he perceived to be the gulf between full-time officials and their mass membership, Goldstein described the T&G as 'an oligarchy at every level of its structures, failing to elicit the active participation of its members'.[4] In his view, shop stewards needed to become more formally integrated in the union's structures if this gap between the leader and the rank and file were to be bridged. But this had not been Bevin's take.

Bevin's leadership has already been described as authoritarian, if not actually autocratic. Andrew Murray quotes a left-wing historian as concluding that Bevin 'enjoyed power blatantly and (he was) as ruthless as Stalin with his opponents'.[5] Deakin inherited Bevin's control freakery, if not his more particular understanding of working-class struggle. He seems to have thought that apathy on the part of the membership meant that all was going well, in fact, although he did also worry that communists might take advantage of such a situation. So firm management was needed, in Deakin's view, in order to nip such possibilities in the bud.

Deakin's regular contributions to the T&G's *The Record* illustrate these concerns, on a continuing basis. As *The Record* quoted him as saying to a T&G event in Plymouth for example: 'I am not in a position to dictate to the Executive'.[6] 'How can one man dictate to thirty-nine others? But as General Secretary it is my duty to give that leadership which is right

---

1 Hutt, *British Trade Unionism* (1975), p.91.

2 Murray, *The T&G Story*.

3 Murray, *The T&G Story*, p.45.

4 Joseph Goldstein, *The Government of British Trade Unions* (Allen & Unwin, 1952), p.271.

5 Murray, *The T&G Story*, p.81.

6 Arthur Deakin, *The Record*, April 1950, p.289.

and proper' including taking 'a very definite line on Communism'. Any challenges to his leadership on the basis that there was a democratic deficit within the T&G tended to be met in similar vein – any such challengers must be mistaken and/or misguided if not actually communist stooges.

Writing in January 1950 in similar vein, Deakin replied to what he considered to have been a challenge to democracy within the T&G.

> For the second time within three months [presumably referring to debates on the bans and proscriptions on communists and fascists, agreed at the BDC in 1949] Communist technique has been used in an attempt to interfere with the administration of the Union [...]. The disgusting attempt by some 180 people, claiming to be members of the Union, to force the General Executive Council, at its December meeting, to meet a deputation organised by a group calling itself 'Committee for Trade Union Democracy' inspired by members of the Communist Party was clearly an attempt to abuse and intimidate the General Executive Council and prevent them from applying the decision reached by the rank-and-file delegates at the 1949 Biennial Delegate Conference [...]. We cannot afford to allow our Trade Union Movement to be exploited by people who, either willingly or unwillingly, are stooges of international Communism.[7]

As Deakin reiterated when addressing T&G members in the West Country a couple of months later, 'the Communists have set up a committee, to restore democracy to the Union'. 'We shall watch this position and take appropriate action'.[8] Challenges to the adequacy – or otherwise – of the T&G's democratic procedures were not going to be permitted on Deakin's watch. He subsequently referred to the Dockers' Charter – for Dockers' rights – as yet another example of communist manipulation, 'the exploitation of industrial grievances to achieve political ends', the 'achievement of Communist domination of the British Trade Union Movement'.[9]

Nor was Deakin inclined to brook criticism from any other quarter. In an interview with Louise Brodie for an oral history project, Geoffrey Goodman recounted a meeting with Deakin, when he had been working as a journalist for the (Labour supporting) *News Chronicle*.[10] There had been industrial unrest in the docks which Geoffrey Goodman set in the context

---

7 Deakin, *The Record*, 1950, p.206.
8 Deakin, *The Record*, 1950, p.265.
9 Deakin, *The Record*, 1950, p.126.
10 Louise Brodie, 'Interview with Goodman, Geoffrey (5 of 9). Oral History of the British Press' (2008), https://sounds.bl.uk/Oral-history/Press-and-media/021M-C0638X0016XX-0005V0.

of the existence of malpractices within the union. There had been allegations of election fiddles and money changing hands. Deakin's response was
to have Geoffrey Goodman thrown out of his office.

Deakin has been described as an awkward, intolerant man who was
resolutely determined to exercise control from the top down. During his
time in office he increased the number of full-time officials significantly,
from around 500 during the war years, to nearly 1,500 (1,434) by 1954,
aiming to exercise tight control over their operations in the field. Unofficial
actions were to be strictly curtailed. He had already described unofficial
action in the Meat Transport organisation at Smithfield Market as both
'unpleasant and disastrous',[11] unofficial strikes – or indeed any kind of
strike – as being a luxury that could not be afforded at the time.

This was an objective that was to prove easier said than done however,
even when officials tried to carry out his bidding, as Chapter 2 has already
outlined. Whether in the docks or road haulage, the motor industry or on
the buses, conflicts continued to erupt from the bottom up. Reflecting on
the experiences of the London busmen's struggles, Bob Potter suggested
that '[m]uch of the responsibility for the worsening conditions must be
placed on bad trade union leadership' going on to argue that 'Deakin
was more interested in hunting Communists than in fighting for his
membership'.[12]

Deakin didn't have it all his own way, however, as previous chapters
have illustrated. Both his successors, Frank Cousins and Jack Jones, gave
him grief during their times as officials during the Deakin era, clearly
demonstrating their own understandings of local situations and grievances
and their readiness to support industrial action where needed, in response.
It was ironic perhaps that Frank Cousins went on to experience his
own problems with officials, so many of whom had been appointed and
schooled in the ways of the Deakin era.

There were further ironies too, as the previous chapter has already
outlined, in terms of Deakin's support for trade union education within
the T&G. His enthusiasm for educating shop stewards may have stemmed
from his overall approach, envisaging education as a mechanism for
managing rank-and-file militancy, focusing shop stewards' minds on the
nuts and bolts of their roles and responsibilities on the shop floor. But
trade union education was indeed like 'casting bread on the waters', with
unanticipated results, contributing to shop stewards' enhanced status,
shifting the balance of power for the coming period.

Frank Cousins, Deakin's successor as general secretary, had a very
different approach to the question of democracy within the T&G. Andrew
Murray has summarised their different contributions as follows: 'no leader

11 Deakin, *The Record*, 1950, p.74.
12 Bob Potter, *London Busmen in Battle* (Pamphlet MML, 1958).

Figure 10: Frank Cousins, a democratic approach to leadership

changed the union more than Cousins'. Whilst Bevin had built the union up it was Cousins who 'altered the balance between officials' opinions and members desires in favour of the latter'. In addition to his wider political contributions, Frank Cousins 'breathed life into its atrophied democracy'. He 'began the policy of pushing power downwards and outwards from the centre of the union', Murray continues. 'Regions gained authority at the expense of national officials and Central Office'.[13]

Frank Cousins has already been quoted as pointing out that the fact that 'he believed in democracy' was justification for supporting industrial

13 Murray, *The T&G Story*, p.135.

action, despite his own personal reservations about the members' chances of winning the particular dispute in question. He clearly did respect members' views and took account of them as he demonstrated by his sensitivity, taking account of dissenting views on the question of nuclear weapons during the biennial conference in the Isle of Man in 1959 (outlined in Chapter 3).

As Frank Cousins himself expressed when addressing trade union members in Coventry in 1956 (warning of the threat to full employment that was being posed by the government's economic policies), the union would face these threats by continuing 'to act as a team' in response. This was 'because it is based on the fundamental principle that its organisation is responsible to the membership through its lay and full-time officers'.[14]

He was also personally committed to equalities agendas, as Chapter 4 outlined, even if the T&G still had a mountain to climb, when it came to the representation of women and Black and minority ethnic members on key decision-making structures. Photos of the GECs of this period were still predominantly male and white.

But this is in no way to downplay his achievements, as a whole. Summarising his time in office before his retirement Frank Cousins explained that:

> When I arrived, I found a trade union 'establishment' very firmly in control. These people believed absolutely in imposing decisions from the top [...] Now thirteen years later much of the apathy that marked official trade unionism has disappeared. There is more freedom, more open-mindedness and ordinary workers are increasingly being encouraged to demand, and to get, a bigger say in the running of their own unions and the industries in which they work.[15]

Democracy in the Workplace

This brings the discussion to the question of democracy in the workplace itself. During the Second World War, as Andrew Murray's history of the T&G explains, workers had been involved in planning and organising production for the first time in Britain's industrial history through joint production committees. These were to boost production while entrenching trade union and workers' rights, potentially putting trade unions on a par with the government and employers alike. Bevin has already been quoted as claiming that the TUC had virtually become part of the state,

---

14 Frank Cousins, in *The Record* (T&G, 1956), p.42.
15 Murray, *The T&G Story*, p.136–137.

making its views heard at the highest levels. Whether or not this reflected Bevin's corporatist aspirations, rather than describing the actual reality, is another question. The point was that expectations had been raised. Trade unions had supported the war effort, gaining experience of planning and organising production in the process, just as the Labour Party had gained experience of government, participating in the wartime coalition. Change was firmly on the agenda from the trade union and labour movement's point of view. No return to the bad old days of the thirties, it was hoped, and indeed expected. As John Price, the head of the T&G's political department had argued back in 1940: 'Organised labour will henceforth be satisfied with nothing less than full partnership in the state'.[16]

Nationalisation was central to these post-war strategies for change, as the 1945 Labour manifesto 'Let us face the future' had outlined. The Attlee government's nationalisation programme had included the railways, coal, gas and electricity, most (but not all) wharves and docks, London's buses and tubes, and the Bank of England. Taken together with the establishment of the NHS and the post-war welfare state, this was a truly momentous programme. But what did these changes actually mean in practice in terms of more effective democratic accountability, let alone workers' control? Who would actually be making the key decisions, at what level, and in whose interests?

The boards of the newly nationalised industries were to be appointed by the relevant minister, modelled on Herbert Morrison's scheme for London Transport. Board members were to be selected on the basis of their management competence, the business efficiency model of nationalisation, as Chapter 1 outlined. This was not about the promotion of industrial democracy per se. On the contrary in fact. As Shinwell, the Minister for Fuel and Power, emphasised in 1946, 'we must employ the best man [*sic*] for the job'.[17]

A number of trade union functionaries were, in fact, offered positions when these boards were constituted, as in the case of the National Dock Labour Corporation, for example. But as Ken Coates went on to point out, they 'were expected to sever their direct trade union connections and were in no way accountable to their former memberships'.[18] They were accountable upwards rather than downwards, in other words, a formula that met with some considerable criticism although to no avail. Whilst celebrating the achievements of Labour in power, R. H. Tawney reflected that 'it did little to remove from wage earners the sense that they belong to a class to be treated as instruments for ends dictated from above'.[19] 'Future

---

16 John Price, *Labour in the War* (Penguin, 1940), p.173.

17 Ken Coates, 'The Vagaries of Participation, 1945–1960', in Ben Pimlott and Chris Cook (eds), *Trade Unions in British Politics* (Longmans, 1982), pp.171–187, p.182.

18 Coates, 'The Vagaries of Participation', p.182.

19 Coates, 'The Vagaries of Participation', p.182.

Labour governments', in Tawney's view, 'must use the industries in public ownership as a laboratory where different methods of making industrial democracy are tested'.[20]

So how were these new structures working out in practice? Early experiences had not been entirely encouraging from the relevant workforces' perspectives, as described in Chapter 2. The National Dock Labour Corporation which had been set up in 1941 had addressed the problem of casualisation in the docks, which was definitely to be welcomed, described by Bevin at the time as a form of workers' control, with the trade union organisations acting jointly with representative employers. The workers themselves expressed very different views subsequently, however. Far from feeling empowered, rank-and-file dock workers described their experiences of feeling that an onerous level of labour discipline had been imposed. This was 'like living under the Gestapo' in their view. There were subsequent criticisms that trade union representation on such boards had actually turned into benefits for those concerned, regardless of their pasts, 'well-feathered nests for the tyrants of the past' as George Brown subsequently described this.[21]

Workers' control was not exactly what the Attlee government had in mind after the war, in any case, as it has already been suggested. Stafford Cripps was on record in 1946 as saying that '[t]here is not yet a very large number of workers in Britain capable of taking over large enterprises [...] Until there have been more workers on the managerial side of industry, I think it would be almost impossible to have worker-controlled industry in Britain, even if it were on the whole desirable'.[22] To be fair, as has also been pointed out in a previous chapter, Cripps was similarly sceptical about the level of competence to be found on the management side. Overall, there were anxieties about the potential for state planning effectively at all, in fact, whoever was doing this.

Such anxieties may well have increased as the Attlee government grappled with the realities of implementation in the immediate post-war period, faced with continuing shortages and economic crises looming on the horizon. The historian Peter Hennessy argues that there had been such difficulties in setting up and running the newly nationalised industries that many of Attlee's ministers lost whatever zest they might have initially felt for 'this element in the socialist transformation'.[23] Even Nye Bevan was for consolidation rather than further nationalisations, in 1950, it seems, although he was passionately in favour of nationalising iron and steel as an exception.

20 R.H. Tawney, *The Radical Tradition* (Pelican, 1966), p.185.
21 Ken Coates and Anthony Topham (eds) *Industrial Democracy and Industrialization*, (Spokesman, 1975), p.59.
22 Hennessy, *Never Again* (2006), p.201.
23 Hennessy, *Never Again*, (2006), p.208.

Although this continued to be contested, further nationalisation continued to be key to socialists' visions however, both then and subsequently throughout this period. Frank Cousins and Jack Jones were both committed to further nationalisations, taking control of the commanding heights of the economy, just as they were both firmly committed to workplace democracy within the nationalised industries and beyond. But theirs was far from being the only view. Left critics have pointed out that others had far more limited views on the issue of nationalisation.

Ralph Miliband was one such critic. He was of the view that the Conservatives had few problems with the Attlee government's approach to nationalisation. Although ultimate control was vested in the minister, with some formal provisions for democratic accountability, he wrote, the reality was actually very different. This conception of public ownership 'ensured the predominance on the boards of the nationalised corporations of men who had been, or who still were, closely associated with private finance and industry, and who could hardly be expected to regard the nationalised industries as designed to achieve any purpose other than the more efficient servicing of the "private sector"'.[24]

Miliband was right to see the debate on the nationalisation of iron and steel as a crucial turning point here in the trajectory of the first Attlee government, Hennessy continued. The nationalisation of iron and steel was very controversial, this being an industry which was seen as potentially profitable at the time rather than an industry in need of rescue by the state. Some of the main proponents of public ownership were in any case beginning to go off the idea, in his view, by 1947, with so many challenges in the post-war period. It became widely assumed that steel would be the government's last measure of public ownership, he concluded.

Iron and steel were subsequently denationalised as it turned out. But debates on nationalisation continued within the trade union and labour movement right through this period and beyond, continuing through to the present day. Nationalisation was seen by its supporters as central to the advance of socialism, taking democratic control over the commanding heights of the economy, the position that was exemplified by debates on Clause 4 and the battle for the soul of the Labour Party at the end of this period (1960).

Meanwhile debates on industrial democracy continued in parallel – and subsequently. Jack Jones was a member of the Committee of Inquiry on Industrial Democracy chaired by Lord Bullock that reported in 1977, a report that provided clear summaries of the different positions that were being put forward to make the case for industrial democracy across

24 Hennessy, *Never Again*, (2006), p.201.

Subsequent Reflections from a T&G Representative on the National Galvanising Board of British Steel

The representative had been an active trade unionist from the time when he had joined the industry, becoming a senior convenor at a very young age. So, he was well positioned to take on this particular role. Although he had so much trade union experience however, he wasn't offered any specific training. This was less than helpful, as he explained more fully subsequently.

The Context in British Steel

British Steel had had a history of experimenting with worker directors in the post-war period when the industry had been relatively successful. By the mid-1970s however, the steel industry had been undergoing processes of contraction, with huge closures. So, the company had decided to set up a joint board with members from both senior management and the trade union side. The aim was to identify investment opportunities to create jobs to replace the jobs that were being lost (and so to ease the processes of industrial change).

The chairman of the British Steel Corporation had been effectively resistant to trade union contributions however, and was someone who had just blithely assumed that everyone would be in agreement with his proposals. This seemed a typical example of 'industrial democracy' from above, in other words, illustrating precisely why trade unionists had expressed reservations about such initiatives coming down from their managements.

Experiences on the Board

Initially this has been a disappointing experience, unsurprisingly given the top-down nature of the processes involved. The representative had also felt hampered by the fact that he had received no formal training – or even briefings – before taking up his position on the board. And there were no formal mechanisms for reporting back to the membership either (although he himself did report back regularly because that was how he believed that representatives should be accountable to their memberships).

Decisions seemed to have been all wrapped up before board meetings. The chairman would put forward plans and just assume that they would go through on the nod. He seemed genuinely surprised when the T&G representative challenged him on this and asked for a vote, as he became more confident about how to intervene in these meetings most effectively.

Despite these unpromising beginnings though, the T&G representative went on to explain that they had eventually managed to make the board useful in practice. The trade union side had found ways to put forward their own ideas about which firms to encourage to invest in the area – firms where it would be possible to promote trade unionism. The local authorities had also been involved in positive ways, working with local trade union representatives as well as with management in the companies that were coming into the area. Overall, he was clear that they had made a difference as a result, encouraging companies to come and invest in the area in order to create decent quality, unionised jobs. But this had all needed more financial support than the government of the day had been prepared to give.

The T&G representative went on to reflect on his experiences on the board compared with his experiences of trade union involvement more generally. He explained that at the local level, trade unions had actually had a great deal of say in how the works had been managed. For example, the trade unions had managed the allocation of overtime, as well as managing cover for sickness arrangements and opportunities for promotion. This could ensure fairness (with no scapegoating of trade union activists). Overall in fact, this had been a good industry to work in with decent wages and conditions generally. But this was not to last.

Much of the steel industry could have been saved in his view, although he recognised that this had been a difficult period with increasing competition from Russia and China, where there were governments that *were* prepared to invest in the industry. But this was absolutely not what the Thatcher government was prepared to do. On the contrary in fact. The 1979/1980 strike marked a turning point here. The strike was called off in 1980 at which point Margaret Thatcher ended worker involvement structures for good.

The loss of the steel industry had had devastating effects on the area in South Wales. The area had been wrecked. But the future could have been otherwise. Parts of the steel industry could have been saved. And the trade unions could have played major roles in the process. Whatever the limitations, in his view, worker representation on boards could have positive benefits. But that was not to be in the steel industry from the Thatcher years.

sectors.[25] The economic case was summarised in terms of the need to get employees on side in order to minimise resistance to industrial change. The experiences of successful competitor countries such as West Germany and Sweden demonstrated that having employee representatives on company boards could contribute to 'avoiding the industrial conflict which has cost Britain so dear'.[26] Far from obstructing change and causing unnecessary delays, as many employers feared, the case for industrial democracy

25 Cmnd 6706, Report of the Committee of Inquiry on Industrial Democracy (HMSO, 1977).
26 Cmnd 6706, p.25.

was being promoted to 'improve efficiency [...] developing new forms of co-operation between capital and labour and a new legitimacy for the exercise of the management function', enabling changes to be implemented without 'costly industrial disputes and loss of production'.[27]

This was precisely why there were reservations from the trade union and labour movement. There were fears that collective bargaining could be undermined, along with fears that trade union representatives would have to participate in unpopular decisions and so lose the confidence of the workers that they were supposed to be representing. Despite such all too understandable reservations, there were continuing aspirations for the promotion of industrial democracy, however, along with continuing aspirations for further nationalisation to take control of the commanding heights of the economy. Although the following account refers to a slightly later period, this does illustrate some of the inherent tensions as well as the more positive possibilities of workers' involvement in these ways.

Debates Within the T&G

There had been debates on nationalisation and workers' control within the union in parallel with wider debates, as exemplified by motions passed at T&G biennial conferences. In 1957 for instance, Conference passed a motion in support of the public ownership of industry adding that 'full advantage should be taken of the knowledge, skill and experience of the workers and that in appointments made in the industries concerned regard should be paid to those whose training, background and experience are of such character as to fit the to undertake the responsibilities of management'[28] – supported with relevant training. The motion was passed unanimously. The following biennial conference (in Douglas, the Isle of Man in 1959) passed a similar motion, reaffirming belief in the extension of the principle of nationalisation 'in order to secure the socialistic principle of control of production and distribution in the national interest'.[29] Managers in nationalised industries should be committed to making them work and there should be 'a greater degree of effective workers' participation in management and control in nationalised industries'.[30]

Addressing the Institute of Directors in 1956, Frank Cousins emphasised the potential for building on the provisions for joint negotiation

---

27 Cmnd 6706, p.49.

28 MRC MSS.126/TG/1887/17. Record of the 17th Biennial Delegate Conference, 1957.

29 MRC MSS.126/TG/1887/18. Record of the 18th Biennial Delegate Conference, 1959.

30 MRC MSS.126/TG/1887/18. Record of the 18th Biennial Delegate Conference, 1959.

that had been established during the Second World War when 'the road was opened to a situation in which workers had for the first time, a real opportunity to control their working life, and a real chance to contribute to industry not merely with their physical strength and skill, but their ideas and personal qualities also'.[31] This was potentially revolutionary. But joint machineries could only work if employers didn't just see them as mechanisms for getting their own policies carried out, he continued. This was the type of approach to industrial democracy that was being debated within the T&G, under his leadership.

Both biennial conferences provided additional evidence of the shifts that had taken place within the T&G, by the end of this period, under the leadership of Frank Cousins as general secretary. The union's progressive support for nationalisation and industrial democracy was mirrored by its support for peace, equalities and international solidarity. From 1955 onwards conferences had also reaffirmed their opposition to racial discrimination (although there were reservations about imported labour). They had consistently supported equal pay for equal work for women (a continuing struggle still very much needing to be taken further, as Volume 4 goes on to explain). And they had expressed solidarity with political and trade union leaders engaged in struggles for freedom and democracy elsewhere, whether in Africa (1955) or in Cyprus (1957) – calling for acceptance of the right to self-determination for the people of Cyprus, for example.

The 1959 biennial conference in Douglas, Isle of Man was also the conference that affirmed the T&G's support for 'the complete and permanent cessation by Great Britain of the testing of Nuclear Weapons', with neither 'Nuclear bombs or rockets with nuclear warheads to be used first by Great Britain or from our territory'.[32] This was a moral question as well as a political one, Frank Cousins argued, summarising the progressive stance that the union was now taking. In summary then, by the end of the fifties, with Frank Cousins as general secretary, the T&G was taking the lead in the battle for the soul of the Labour Party and the wider trade union and labour movement, supporting movements for peace and democratic freedom in Britain and beyond, internationally.

31 Cousins, *The Record*, p.179.
32 MRC MSS.126/TG/1887/18. Record of the 18th Biennial Delegate Conference, 1959.

Concluding Questions

This takes the discussion back to the questions that have framed this volume's account of the T&G's history during this post-war period, asking what we can learn through:

- reflecting on past experiences of class struggles, including international experiences of solidarity

- reflecting on struggles for democracy and equalities both within the trade union movement and within the wider social context

- reflecting on relationships between trade unions, employers and the state, with a particular focus on relationships with the Labour Party more specifically

- drawing lessons from past achievements and mistakes to apply these critically to contemporary challenges, recognising past shortcomings as well as celebrating past achievements

What else might be learnt, in addition, about the ways in which the T&G was transformed between 1945 and 1960? And how could the achievements of this period enable the union to take on the challenges that were to follow, from the sixties onwards?

Index